TIME TO LAUGH

Children—and grownups, too—love to laugh. Their sense of humor and appreciation of "the ridiculous" is keen, and the chuckles and shouts of laughter with which they greet "funny stories" are contagious.

To meet the steady demand for just such stories, Phyllis Fenner has collected twenty of the most outstanding tales, favorites of yesterday and of today; tales our grandmothers read to us, at which we chortled in delight, and which are proving just as popular with our own children and grandchildren.

Time to Laugh

Time to Laugh

FUNNY TALES FROM HERE AND THERE

SELECTED BY

PHYLLIS R. FENNER

Illustrated by Henry C. Pitz

NEW YORK · ALFRED · A · KNOPF

HOW PAT GOT GOOD SENSE, copyright 1940 by Story Parade.
THE DEVIL'S HIDE, copyright 1922 by Parker Fillmore.
MR. A. AND MR. P., copyright 1932 by Margery Williams Bianco.
THE SIMPLETON AND HIS LITTLE BLACK HEN, copyright 1887 by Harper & Brothers, copyright 1915 by Anne Poole Pyle.
CONAL AND DONAL AND TAIG, copyright 1900 by McClure, Phillips & Co.
THE DRAWBRIDGE, copyright 1939 by Coward-McCann, Inc.
BABY RAINSTORM, copyright 1940 by Story Parade.
THE LAUGHING PRINCE, copyright 1921 by Parker Fillmore.
AH MEE'S INVENTION, copyright 1925 by E. P. Dutton & Company, Inc.
THE GHOST'S GHOST, copyright 1939 by Random House, Inc.
THE THREE INNKEEPERS, copyright 1932 by Harper & Brothers.
ABOUT ELIZABETH ELIZA'S PIANO, copyright 1886 by Ticknor & Co., copyright 1914 by Ellen Day Hale, copyright 1924 by Houghton Mifflin Company.
THE PETERKINS TRY TO BECOME WISE, copyright 1886 by Ticknor & Co., copyright 1914 by Ellen Day Hale, copyright 1924 by Houghton Mifflin Company.
GUDBRAND ON THE HILL-SIDE, copyright 1917 by G. P. Putnam's Sons.
RATS, copyright 1938 by J. B. S. Haldane.
THE PALACE ON THE ROCK, copyright 1940 by Harper & Brothers.
JUAN CIGARRON, copyright 1941 by Story Parade.
EBENEZER NEVER-COULD-SNEEZER, copyright 1936 by Story Parade.
THE WEE RED MAN, copyright 1926 by Frederick A. Stokes Company.

TO

FRANCIS

remembering the time he *laughed*
at

THE WEE RED MAN

GET READY TO

LAUGH

IN DIFFERENT PARTS of the world people wear different kinds of clothes, eat different foods, talk different tongues, but everywhere people "laugh in the same language." Everywhere people love to laugh at the stupid fellow who does the wrong thing, at the boy who fools his smart brothers, at sheer nonsense, at incongruities, at exaggeration.

Wherever people live, laughing makes them feel better, gives them courage, unity, strength, just as those in *The Laughing Prince* "found that they were working all the better for their jollity." And it would be a better world if, as in Stefan's kingdom, "laughter grew fashionable." Of course, there will always be people who, like Stefan's two brothers, "tried to take up laughing but couldn't do very well at it," but they'd be the better for the trying.

Have a good laugh now, with Pat, and stupid Caspar, and the Finnish boy who beat the devil; at

Mouseknees and his troubles, at the Peterkin family, at Conal O'Donnell, and the others. They have made folks laugh the world over. So get ready! for they're bound to get a laugh out of you.

P.R.F.

CONTENTS

HOW PAT GOT GOOD SENSE   3
by Charles J. Finger

THE DEVIL'S HIDE   17
by Parker Fillmore

MR. A AND MR. P   36
by Margery Bianco

THE SIMPLETON AND
  HIS LITTLE BLACK HEN   44
by Howard Pyle

CONAL AND DONAL AND TAIG   58
by Seumas MacManus

THE DRAWBRIDGE   67
by Lesley Frost

BABY RAINSTORM   74
by Glen Rounds

Contents]

THE LAUGHING PRINCE   85
     by Parker Fillmore

THE EMPEROR'S NEW CLOTHES   108
     by Hans Christian Andersen

AH MEE'S INVENTION   116
     by Arthur Bowie Chrisman

THE GHOST'S GHOST   127
     by William C. White

THE THREE INNKEEPERS *or* THE
   KING'S LEGS   150
     by Richard Hughes

ABOUT ELIZABETH ELIZA'S
   PIANO   159
     by Lucretia P. Hale

THE PETERKINS TRY TO BECOME
   WISE   163
     by Lucretia P. Hale

GUDBRAND ON THE HILL-SIDE   168
     by G. W. Dasent

RATS   175
     by J. B. S. Haldane

THE PALACE ON THE ROCK   192
     by Richard Hughes

JUAN CIGARRON   200
     by Ruth Sawyer

EBENEZER NEVER-COULD-
   SNEEZER   209
     by Gilbert S. Pattillo

THE WEE RED MAN   217
     by Seumas MacManus

Time to Laugh

How Pat Got Good Sense

Pat was a lad who was always ready to laugh, even at himself, and he was willing to lend a hand when any one asked him. The only trouble with him was that while he could put two and two together as well as the next, he often put them together at the wrong time. For instance, see how it was when he went to work for Farmer O'Grady.

"Take the dog," says the farmer, "and gather the sheep on yon hill side and put them through the gate into the meadow beyond."

"Sure, I'll do it and just as you say," answered Pat.

So Pat took a rope and tied it to the dog's neck and went dragging the dog after him, the dog mighty annoyed, too. Indeed, never was a better sheep dog, but there he was at the end of a rope being dragged up hill and down, with the lad at the other end of the rope, shouting at the sheep and taking an hour to do what the dog could do in five minutes.

Pat, with the dog still on the rope, was taking a drink at the pump when O'Grady came up.

"A fine to-do," says O'Grady, "all that leg work for nothing."

" 'Twas the dog that made most of the trouble," says Pat.

"Trouble, indeed," says O'Grady. "By the Great Horn Spoon, it's you who made the trouble, dragging a good dog at the rope's end when a word would have sent the dog to do the job for you."

"Didn't you say, 'Take the dog?' " answered Pat. "And how could I take it and send it, too?"

"You're right there," said O'Grady. "However, it's as well to remember that four legs can travel faster than two."

"I'll remember and thank you kindly," says Pat.

"There's nothing much to do till meal time except odd jobs, so you may as well amuse yourself doing them," says O'Grady.

So Pat did nothing much except pull weeds, carry wood and water to the house, clean the pig pen, gather peat, sweep the chicken house, dig potatoes, tidy the barn loft, run messages for the housewife and do what Betty the maid told him. So the time passed quickly, and Pat had an appetite and was ready for the noon meal when O'Grady came up.

"There's nothing like exercise before meals," says the farmer. "Do you, while you're waiting for dinner, run into the village and bring out a table the carpenter has made by my order."

"With all the good will in the world," says Pat and off he went at a lively trot down the dusty road. The carpenter was just going to his dinner when he arrived, but there was the table ready. So, in a couple of minutes Pat was on his way to the farm with the table on his back, and a clumsy load it was. After a mile Pat sat down to rest in the shade of a big tree. Then it was that an idea struck him.

"Why," says he, "the table's got four legs, and what did Mister O'Grady tell me but that a thing with four legs could travel faster than two legs. So we'll see how that works out."

With that off went Pat at a good clip, hungry for

his dinner, and got to the farm house just when Betty was clearing away the dinner things.

"And where's the table?" asked O'Grady.

"It's on the road and will soon be here," answered Pat, then told how things were.

"Ochone!" says O'Grady when he heard the story. "Was there ever such a fellow! What I had in mind when I spoke about a thing with four legs was a dog, or a horse, or a rabbit. Well, what you don't have in your head, you'll have to have in your heels. So back you go and bring the table home, and next time put two and two together. You should have hitched the horse to the cart and carried the table that way."

"Thank you," said Pat. "I'll remember next time. But how about dinner?"

"Hunger is the best sauce," says O'Grady. "When you get back you'll have a fine appetite."

So off went Pat, found the table where he had left it, carried it to the farm, sat down to the scraps of dinner that were left, and played a very good knife and fork, as the saying is. But no sooner had he finished than Betty the maid came running.

"There's never a match in the house," says she. "Do you, like a good lad, run to the village and bring a box."

"Nothing could please me better than pleasing you," says he, and off he went to the stable where he put harness on the horse, put the horse in the shafts, and drove to the village, as happy a lad as ever whistled a tune. Then he put the box of matches in the cart and drove back singing merrily, picking up a beggar man on the road.

"And, now, what's this. What's this?" asked O'Grady when he saw Pat drive up with the beggar man and the matches.

"Didn't you tell me to take the horse and cart?" answered Pat.

"And what's your pocket for?" asked O'Grady.

"I see. I see," said Pat. "I'll do it next time."

"You'll get sense knocked into your head some day," says O'Grady. "In the meanwhile get busy."

So Pat turned the hay, fed the pigs, tended a sick cow, chopped down and chopped up a dead oak, dug a ditch at the pigsty and was wondering when all the odd jobs would be done when Betty came.

"Run like a good lad," says she, "over to Farmer Murphy's place. Tell him to let us have a pint of honey and be quick about it."

Off went Pat and found Farmer Murphy sitting in the shade. When Pat had told his message, Farmer Murphy said, "Go, Pat, to the milk house and take what you need."

Now, what with butter, milk, cheese and apples, Pat found the milk house a good place to be in. So he drank his fill of milk, ate a slice of cheese, munched a couple of apples, and then found the honey.

" 'Tis a good man who tells me to take what I need," said Pat. "And lucky a lad am I to have a pocket for the honey as Farmer O'Grady told me." With that he poured the honey into his trouser pocket and turned his face farmwards, as happy a lad as ever whistled a tune. But a terrible pother there was when he got to the kitchen door with nothing to show but a wet and sticky pocket. And when the farmer's wife saw how matters were, she set up a scream that brought Farmer O'Grady.

"Now, I begin to believe that if you had a staircase in front of you, you'd look for a rope to go down it," said he. "Anyway, 'tis a long road that has no turn, and you'll get sense knocked into you some day. Why didn't you take a jar and put the honey in that? You ought to have thought that honey runs when you pour it, so a jar would be better than your pocket to carry it home."

"True enough," said Pat. "I'll think of that next time."

So the farmer went one way and Pat another, and Pat's job was working round the house, piling firewood and peat, cleaning out the rain barrel, splitting kindling wood, cleaning out the attic and, also, cleaning out the dog house. While he was doing the last, Betty came and said, "Now, Pat, never was there a better working lad than you."

"Thank you kindly," says Pat, "but too much praise is a burden. What is it you want me to do now?"

"Why," says she, "there's a puppy over at O'Brien's which was promised me. Do you run over and get it."

"If 'twould please you, 'twould delight me," says Pat.

"If you hurry you'll be back by pudding time," says she.

Off went Pat and when he was at the O'Brien place he found the farmer unloading hay from his wagon.

When Pat told his message, Farmer O'Brien pointed to the dog house, told Pat to help himself, then drove away to the stable.

"Now," says Pat, "let me do the errand right. It's got four legs but I can't tell it to go where it ought to go because I can't tell it the way. I can't carry it in the wagon because there's never a wagon here. I can't put it in my pocket because never a pocket have I that is large enough. But it can run, and, sure enough, Farmer O'Grady says, says he, 'When anything runs, put it in a jar.' "

So Pat found a jar, put the pup in it, clapped on the top and went his way singing and whistling.

And "O, whirra! whirra! what shall I do with a

dead dog," cried Betty when she found the puppy in the jar, dead as could be.

"Send the lad about his business and tell him never to show his face here again," said the housewife. "Such a fellow would try to lock a door with a boiled carrot," she went on, her voice getting higher and higher, and her face redder and redder. "He's silly enough to try to carry water in a basket."

"Well, wife, the wisest are not always wise," said the farmer. "What you should have done, Pat, was to tie a string to it and lead it, saying, 'Come on, little fellow. Come on.' "

"There's a lot to learn in the world and I thank you," said Pat.

"You'll get sense knocked into your head some day," said the farmer.

So Pat went to work again on this and that, going down into the well to get a bucket that had been dropped, carrying stones to mend a hole in the road, driving a pig out of the turnip patch, trimming a hedge, clearing a nettle patch out of the garden, cutting down briars from behind the cow-house and driving up the cows to be milked.

It was while Pat was milking the cows that Betty came and said, "Do you, Pat, run over the hill to the O'Leary place, and bring back a shin of beef to make soup for tomorrow."

"Nothing would please me better," said Pat and off he went.

"Go and cut what you need," said O'Leary when Pat had told his tale. And a fine joint of beef it was that Pat cut, sure enough. To the shank of it he tied Mrs. O'Leary's clothes line, then went off down the road, singing and whistling, dragging the leg of beef and saying, in a kind voice, "Come on, little fellow. Come on."

And, hearing the call, Connolly's big dog came sniffing after the meat and began to make a running feast of it. And Parnell's hound came too, and Mac-Manus's yellow dog, and O'Connor's white dog. Then other dogs came until a pack of them were following, and still more came as Pat cried, "Come on, little fellow. Come on."

There were ten of them, then a dozen, then a score, and a fine time they had, yelping, biting, barking, snatching at the meat and tearing off great pieces, stealing one from another and going back to get more. There were terriers, bull dogs, hounds; dogs with short legs and dogs with long ones; dogs that were good for sheep and dogs that were good for nothing; pet dogs and dogs that nobody liked; dogs with curly hair and dogs with straight hair and dogs with no hair at all; and every dog had an appetite.

So there was a terrible to-do when Pat and four

dozen dogs got to the farm and nothing was left of the beef but a bone. The farmer's wife was all for sending Pat about his business then and there.

"I tell you he's a fool," says she.

"Well, he isn't all that he might be," said the farmer. "Come to that, neither is anyone of us. Still, he lends a willing hand."

"Sure, there's none without a fault," says Betty, "and while the two of you are talking about him, he might as well run down to the village and get a bag of sugar."

"And you don't need the horse and cart," says the farmer.

"And you don't pour it in your pocket," added Betty. "You carry the sack on your shoulder."

"And you don't let the wild creatures eat up what you ought to eat yourself, like you did with the beef," said the patient O'Grady.

"Sure, and I never make the same mistake twice," said Pat, and off he went. And a fine lad he looked, too, on his way back with the sack of sugar on his shoulder. Whistling and singing, he was, and thinking it a very good world, indeed, since it was as free for a fly as for an eagle. It was while thinking that very thing that he saw how flies by the hundreds were on the sugar sack, and that the sugar was trickling out of a hole. Just then he was passing the school with the children coming out to go home.

"Pat," cried one and the other, "the sugar is leak-ing out."

"Why, so it is," said Pat. "And there's flies helping themselves, sure enough. And didn't Mister O'Grady tell me that the wild creatures should never eat what I ought to eat, myself?"

With that Pat sat down, helped himself to the sugar, called on the young children to help them-selves, and very soon nothing was left but an empty sack.

"Well," says Pat, "at any rate it's all the easier to carry, so I'll get back all the sooner."

Now, to this very day in County Meath they tell of the scolding that Mister O'Grady gave Pat when he got back with the empty sack. The farmer said things that were bad enough, then others that were worse, while Pat sat and listened, so that at last Farmer O'Grady had nothing more to say and felt sorry that he had said so much, and still more sorry for Pat. So, after all that scolding and ranting, and all those hard words, Pat says, easy like, "And what would you have done, sir?"

"What I always do when I see a fly," answered O'Grady.

"And what's that?" asked Pat. "There's one on my head this very moment."

"I always hit it," says O'Grady.

"Then do so," says Pat as he thrust his head forward.

"With all the good will in the world," says O'Grady. With that he gave Pat a clout on the side of the head that killed the fly and made the lad see stars. And, they say, it knocked sense into his head at the same moment.

The Devil's Hide

There was once a Finnish boy who got the best of the Devil. His name was Erkki. Erkki had two brothers who were, of course, older than he. They both tried their luck with the Devil and got the worst of it. Then Erkki tried his luck. They were sure Erkki, too, would be worsted, but he wasn't. Here is the whole story:

One day the oldest brother said:

"It's time for me to go out into the world and earn my living. Do you two younger ones wait here at home until you hear how I get on."

The younger boys agreed to this and the oldest brother started out. He was unable to get employment until by chance he met the Devil. The Devil at once offered him a place but on very strange terms.

"Come work for me," the Devil said, "and I promise that you'll be comfortably housed and well fed. We'll make this bargain: the first of us who loses his temper will forfeit to the other enough of his own hide to sole a pair of boots. If I lose my temper first, you may exact from me a big patch of my hide. If you lose your temper first, I'll exact the same from you."

The oldest brother agreed to this and the Devil at once took him home and set him to work.

"Take this ax," he said, "and go out behind the house and chop me some firewood."

The oldest brother took the ax and went out to the woodpile.

"Chopping wood is easy enough," he thought to himself.

But at the first blow he found that the ax had no edge. Try as he would he couldn't cut a single log.

"I'd be a fool to stay here and waste my time with such an ax!" he cried.

So he threw down the ax and ran away thinking to escape the Devil and get work somewhere else. But the Devil had no intention of letting him escape. He ran after him, overtook him, and asked him what he meant leaving thus without notice.

"I don't want to work for you!" the oldest brother cried, petulantly.

"Very well," the Devil said, "but don't lose your temper about it."

"I will so lose my temper!" the oldest brother declared. "The idea—expecting me to cut wood with such an ax!"

"Well," the Devil remarked, "since you insist on losing your temper, you'll have to forfeit me enough of your hide to sole a pair of boots! That was our bargain."

The oldest brother howled and protested but to no purpose. The Devil was firm. He took out a long knife and slit off enough of the oldest brother's hide to sole a pair of big boots.

"Now then, my boy," he said, "now you may go."

The oldest brother went limping home complaining bitterly at the hard fate that had befallen him.

"I'm tired and sick," he told his brothers, "and I'm going to stay home and rest. One of you will have to go out and work."

The second brother at once said that he'd be de-

lighted to try his luck in the world. So he started out
and he had exactly the same experience. At first he
could get no work, then he met the Devil and the
Devil made exactly the same bargain with him that he
had made with the oldest brother. He took the second
brother home with him, gave him the same dull ax,
and sent him out to the woodpile. After the first stroke
the second brother threw down the ax in disgust and
tried to run off and the Devil, of course, wouldn't let
him go until he, too, had submitted to the loss of a
great patch of hide. So it was no time at all before
the second brother came limping home complaining
bitterly at fate.

"What ails you two?" Erkki said.

"You go out into the cruel world and hunt work,"
they told him, "and you'll find out soon enough
what ails us! And when you do find out you needn't
come limping home expecting sympathy from us for
you won't get it!"

So the very next day Erkki started out, leaving his
brothers at home nursing their sore backs and their
injured feelings.

Well, Erkki had exactly the same experience. At
first he could get work nowhere, then later he met
the Devil and went into his employ on exactly the
same terms as his brothers.

The Devil handed him the same dull ax and sent

him out to the woodpile. At the first blow Erkki knew that the ax had lost its edge and would never cut a single log. But instead of being discouraged and losing his temper, he only laughed.

"I suppose the Devil thinks I'll lose my hide over a trifle like this!" he said. "Well, I just won't!"

He dropped the ax and, going over to the woodpile, began pulling it down. Under all the logs he found the Devil's cat. It was an evil looking creature with a gray head.

"Ha!" thought Erkki, "I bet anything you've got something to do with this!"

He raised the dull ax and with one blow cut off the evil creature's head. Sure enough the ax instantly recovered its edge and after that Erkki had no trouble at all in chopping as much firewood as the Devil wanted.

That night at supper the Devil said:

"Well, Erkki, did you finish the work I gave you?"

"Yes, master, I've chopped all that wood."

The Devil was surprised.

"Really?"

"Yes, master. You can go out and see for yourself."

"Then you found something in the woodpile, didn't you?"

"Nothing but an awful looking old cat."

The Devil started.

"Did you do anything to that cat?"

"I only chopped its head off and threw it away."

"What!" the Devil cried angrily. "Didn't you know that was my cat!"

"There now, master," Erkki said soothingly, "you're not going to lose your temper over a little thing like a dead cat, are you? Don't forget our bargain!"

The Devil swallowed his anger and murmured:

"No, I'm not going to lose my temper but I must say that was no way to treat my cat."

The next day the Devil ordered Erkki to go out to the forest and bring home some logs on the ox sledge.

"My black dog will go with you," he said, "and as you come home you're to take exactly the same course the dog takes."

Well, Erkki went out to the forest and loaded the ox sledge with logs and then drove the oxen home following the Devil's black dog. As they reached the Devil's house the black dog jumped through a hole in the gate.

"I must follow master's orders," Erkki said to himself.

So he cut up the oxen into small pieces and put them through the same hole in the gate; he chopped up the logs and pitched them through the hole; and he broke up the sledge into pieces small enough to follow the oxen and the logs. Then he crept through the hole himself.

That night at supper the Devil said:

"Well, Erkki, did you come home the way I told you?"

"Yes, master, I followed the black dog."

"What!" the Devil cried. "Do you mean to say you brought the oxen and the sledge and the logs through the hole in the gate?"

"Yes, master, that's what I did."

"But you couldn't!" the Devil declared.

"Well, master," Erkki said, "just go out and see."

The Devil went outside and when he saw the method by which Erkki had carried out his orders he was furious. But Erkki quieted him by saying:

"There now, master, you're not going to lose your temper over a trifling matter like this, are you? Remember our bargain!"

"N-n-no," the Devil said, again swallowing his anger, "I'm not going to lose my temper, but I want you to understand, Erkki, that I think you've acted very badly in this!"

All that evening the Devil fumed and fussed about Erkki.

"We've got to get rid of that boy! That's all there is about it!" he said to his wife.

Of course whenever Erkki was in sight the Devil tried to smile and look pleasant, but as soon as Erkki was gone he went back at once to his grievance. He declared emphatically:

"There's no living in peace and comfort with such a boy around!"

"Well," his wife said, "if you feel that way about it, why don't you kill him tonight when he's asleep? We could throw his body into the lake and no one would be the wiser."

"That's a fine idea!" the Devil said. "Wake me up some time after midnight and I'll do it!"

Now Erkki overheard this little plan, so that night he kept awake. When he knew from their snoring that the Devil and his wife were sound asleep, he slipped over to their bed, quietly lifted the Devil's wife in his arms, and without awakening her placed her gently in his own bed. Then he put on some of her clothes and laid himself down beside the Devil in the wife's place.

Presently he nudged the Devil awake.

"What do you want?" the Devil mumbled.

"Sst!" Erkki whispered. "Isn't it time we got up and killed Erkki?"

"Yes," the Devil answered, "it is. Come along."

They got up quietly and the Devil reached down a great sword from the wall. Then they crept over to

Erkki's bed and the Devil with one blow cut off the head of the person who was lying there asleep.

"Now," he said, "we'll just carry out the bed and all and dump it in the lake."

So Erkki took one end of the bed and the Devil the other and, stumbling and slipping in the darkness, they carried it down to the lake and pitched it in.

"That's a good job done!" the Devil said with a laugh.

Then they went back to bed together and the Devil fell instantly asleep.

The next morning when he got up for breakfast, there was Erkki stirring the porridge.

"How—did you get here?" the Devil asked. "I mean—I mean where is my wife?"

"Your wife? Don't you remember," Erkki said, "you cut off her head last night and then we threw her into the lake, bed and all! But no one will be the wiser!"

"W-wh-what!" the Devil cried, and he was about to fly into an awful rage when Erkki restrained him by saying:

"There now, master, you're not going to lose your temper over a little thing like a wife, are you? Remember our bargain!"

So the Devil was forced again to swallow his anger.

"No, I'm not going to lose my temper," he said, "but I tell you frankly, Erkki, I don't think that was a nice trick for you to play on me!"

Well, the Devil felt lonely not having a wife about the house, so in a few days he decided to go off wooing for a new one.

"And, Erkki," he said, "I expect you to keep busy while I'm gone. Here's a keg of red paint. Now get to work and have the house all blazing red by the time I get back."

"All blazing red," Erkki repeated. "Very well, master, trust me to have it all blazing red by the time you get back!"

As soon as the Devil was gone, Erkki set the house afire and in a short time the whole sky was lighted up with the red glow of the flames. In great fright the Devil hurried back and got there in time to see the house one mass of fire.

"You see, master," Erkki said, "I've done as you told me. It looks very pretty, doesn't it? All blazing red!"

The Devil almost choked with rage.

"You—you—" he began, but Erkki restrained him by saying:

"There now, master, you're not going to lose your temper over a little thing like a house afire, are you? Remember our bargain!"

The Devil swallowed hard and said:

"N-no, I'm not going to lose my temper, but I must say, Erkki, that I'm very much annoyed with you!"

The next day the Devil wanted to go awooing again and before he started he said to Erkki:

"Now, no nonsense this time! While I'm gone you're to build three bridges over the lake, but they're not to be built of wood or stone or iron or earth. Do you understand?"

Erkki pretended to be frightened.

"That's a pretty hard task you've given me, master!"

"Hard or easy, see that you get it done!" the Devil said.

Erkki waited until the Devil was gone, then he went out to the field and slaughtered all the Devil's cattle. From the bones of the cattle he laid three bridges across the lake, using the skulls for one bridge, the ribs for another, and the legs and the hoofs for the third. Then when the Devil got back, Erkki met him and pointing to the bridges said:

"See, master, there they are, three bridges put together without stick, stone, iron, or bit of earth!"

When the Devil found out that all his cattle had been slaughtered to give bones for the bridges, he was ready to kill Erkki, but Erkki quieted him by saying:

"There now, master, you're not going to lose your temper over a little thing like the slaughter of a few cattle, are you? Remember our bargain!"

So again the Devil had to swallow his anger.

"No," he said, "I'm not going to lose my temper exactly but I just want to tell you, Erkki, that I don't think you're behaving well!"

The Devil's wooing was successful and pretty soon he brought home a new wife. The new wife didn't like having Erkki about, so the Devil promised her he'd kill the boy.

"I'll do it tonight," he said, "when he's asleep."

Erkki overheard this and that night he put the churn in his bed under the covers, and where his head ordinarily would be he put a big round stone. Then he himself curled up on the stove and went comfortably to sleep.

During the night the Devil took his great sword from the wall and went over to Erkki's bed. His first blow hit the round stone and nicked the sword. His second blow struck sparks.

"Mercy me!" the Devil thought, "he's got a mighty hard head! I better strike lower!"

With the third stroke he hit the churn a mighty blow. The hoops flew apart and the churn collapsed.

The Devil went chuckling back to bed.

"Ha!" he said boastfully to his wife, "I got him that time!"

But the next morning when he woke up he didn't feel like laughing for there was Erkki as lively as ever and pretending that nothing had happened.

"What!" cried the Devil in amazement, "didn't you feel anything strike you last night while you were asleep?"

"Oh, I did feel a few mosquitoes brushing my cheek," Erkki said. "Nothing else."

"Steel doesn't touch him!" the Devil said to his wife. "I think I'll try fire on him."

So that night the Devil told Erkki to sleep in the threshing barn. Erkki carried his cot down to the threshing floor and then when it was dark he shifted it into the hay barn where he slept comfortably all night.

During the night the Devil set fire to the threshing barn. In the early dawn Erkki carried his cot back to the place of the threshing barn and in the morning when the Devil came out the first thing he saw was Erkki unharmed and peacefully sleeping among the smoking ruins.

"Mercy me, Erkki!" he shouted, shaking him awake, "have you been asleep all night?"

"Yes, I've had a fine night's sleep. But I did feel a little chilly."

"Chilly!" the Devil gasped.

After that the Devil's one thought was to get rid of Erkki.

"That boy's getting on my nerves!" he told his wife. "I just can't stand him much longer! What are we going to do about him?"

They discussed one plan after another and at last decided that the only way they'd ever get rid of him would be to move away and leave him behind.

"I'll send him out to the forest to chop wood all day," the Devil said, "and while he's gone we'll row ourselves and all our belongings out to an island and when he comes back he won't know where we've gone."

Erkki overheard this plan and the next day when they were sure he was safely at work in the forest he slipped back and hid himself in the bedclothes.

Well, when they got to the island and began unpacking their things there was Erkki in the bedclothes!

The Devil's new wife complained bitterly.

"If you really loved me," she said, "you'd cut off that boy's head!"

"But I've tried to cut it off!" the Devil declared, "and I never can do it! Plague take such a boy! I've always known the Finns were an obstinate lot but

I must say I've never met one as bad as Erkki! He's too much for me!"

But the Devil's wife kept on complaining until at last the Devil promised that he would try once again to cut off Erkki's head.

"Very well," his wife said, "tonight when he's asleep I'll wake you."

Well, what with the moving and everything the wife herself was tired and as soon as she went to bed she fell asleep. That gave Erkki just the very chance he needed to try on the new wife the trick he had played on the old one. Without waking her he carried her to his bed and then laid himself down in her place beside the Devil. Then he waked up the Devil and reminded him that he had promised to cut off Erkki's head.

The poor old Devil got up and went over to Erkki's bed and of course cut off the head of his new wife.

The next morning when he had found out what he had done, he was perfectly furious.

"You get right out of here, Erkki!" he roared. "I never want to see you again!"

"There now, master," Erkki said, "you're not going to lose your temper over a little thing like a dead wife, are you?"

"I am so going to lose my temper!" the Devil

shouted. "And what's more it isn't a little thing! I liked this wife, I did, and I don't know where I'll get another one I like as well! So you just clear out of here and be quick about it, too!"

"Very well, master," Erkki said, "I'll go but not until you pay me what you owe me."

"What I owe you!" bellowed the Devil. "What about all you owe me for my house and my cattle and my old wife and my dear new wife and everything!"

"You've lost your temper," Erkki said, "and now you've got to pay me a patch of your hide big enough to sole a pair of boots. That was our bargain!"

The Devil roared and blustered but Erkki was firm. He wouldn't budge a step until the Devil had allowed him to slit a great patch of hide off his back.

That piece of the Devil's hide made the finest soles that a pair of boots ever had. It wore for years and years and years. In fact Erkki is still tramping around on those same soles. The fame of them has spread over all the land and it has got so that now people stop Erkki on the highway to look at his wonderful boots soled with the Devil's hide. Travelers from foreign countries are deeply interested when they hear about the boots and when they meet Erkki they question him closely.

"Tell us," they beg him, "how did you get the Devil's hide in the first place?"

Erkki always laughs and makes the same answer:

"I got it by not losing my temper!"

As for the Devil, he's never again made a bargain like that with a Finn!

Mr. A and Mr. P

Of all the storekeepers in town there are none so merry as Mr. A and Mr. P.

They have quite the grandest store on the street. Outside it is painted a bright cheerful red, and inside it is full of all the things that a grocery store should have—soap and crackers and sardines and tubs of butter and red shiny apples, besides shelves and shelves of everything you could possibly think of, all put up in cans.

Mr. A is tall and thin, and Mr. P is short and stout. Mr. A has red hair, and Mr. P has very little hair at all. Mr. A can reach all the things off the top shelves, and Mr. P can get all the things off the bottom shelves. If there is anything on the very top shelf of all, and they have to get the long poker and poke it down, then Mr. A pokes and Mr. P catches, because Mr. P's lap is the widest.

In fact they do everything together. Mr. A takes the money and Mr. P rings the bell. Mr. A counts the groceries, and Mr. P writes them down. Mr. A makes the jokes, and Mr. P laughs at them.

And of an evening, when the store is closed and work is over, then Mr. A plays the flute and Mr. P plays the accordion.

You would think that when two people get along together so well, they would never have a quarrel in the world. But once upon a time they did, and this is how it happened.

For a long time they had been wondering what to do to make their life even merrier than it was. They had tried playing baseball with the soup cans, and football with the watermelons, and building all sorts of castles out of ketchup bottles and breakfast foods, just to see them come tumbling down again. But after a while they got tired of all this, and there just didn't seem anything new to play at.

Then Mr. A had a grand idea. He thought he would change the prices of everything in the store, overnight, just to see how surprised the customers would look when they came around next morning. He didn't want Mr. P to know about it, so that it might be a nice surprise for him, too. For Mr. A was always trying to think of something that would please Mr. P.

But Mr. P, too, was always trying to think of something that would please and surprise Mr. A. And unfortunately he happened to think of exactly the same thing, and he thought of it at almost exactly the same moment as Mr. A.

So each of them, very secretly, set about writing a whole set of new tickets, and each of them, also very secretly, went about sticking the new tickets where they thought it would be most fun.

Mr. A would turn his head suddenly and want to know what Mr. P was giggling about, and Mr. P would stop writing his secret tickets long enough to ask *why* Mr. A was chuckling so, and they would both go off into peals of laughter and then look very solemn and begin working away again faster than ever.

Finally they locked up their store and went home for the night.

The first customer to come next morning was a housewife, and she wanted three cakes of soap for a quarter.

"Twelve cents apiece!" said Mr. A, for he had changed the tickets from the breakfast cereal.

"But they're always three for a quarter," said the housewife.

"Not now, not now!" said Mr. A. "Maybe you're thinking of soup. Soup's three for a quarter. To-day," he added, and then began to giggle. He couldn't help it.

"Why, no it isn't!" cried Mr. P, beginning to giggle too. "It's two for nineteen. Look at that!"

And he winked at Mr. A, but for some reason Mr. A didn't seem to think it was funny at all.

"I tell you it's three for a quarter!" he said indignantly. "The whole week, too!"

"Two for nineteen, two for nineteen!" chanted Mr. P, in an irritating sort of way, and he went about the store humming, "Two for nineteen, two for nineteen!"

"Just like a hen that's laid an egg!" thought Mr. A, beginning to get very annoyed, as people do when their jokes don't turn out to be funny after all.

The next customer wanted sugar and potatoes.

"Six for fifteen!" shouted Mr. P loudly.

"Two for forty-nine!" yelled Mr. A, banging his fist on the counter.

The customers began to get worried. They didn't
know what to make of it at all. And the more Mr. A
chuckled, the madder Mr. P got, and every time Mr.
P giggled, Mr. A was cross enough to bite his head off.

In the afternoon it was worse. No one knew what
anything cost at all. Half the customers were buying
all sorts of things they didn't need just because they
were cheap, and the other half were shouting that
they wanted their money back. As fast as Mr. A stuck
a ticket on one shelf Mr. P tore it down and put a
different one in its place. They kept rushing round
and round the store, doing nothing but change the
tickets, and the last straw was when Mr. A marked
a whole crate of watermelons four for fifteen cents,
and all the boys from the neighborhood came pouring
into the store so fast one couldn't even count them.
And above all the turmoil, and the customers snatching this thing and that—for by this time they were so
confused that they started waiting on one another—
you might hear Mr. A's high squeaky voice shouting,
"Six for nineteen! Six for nineteen, I tell you!" and
Mr. P's deep bass rumbling, "Three for a quarter!"

It was like a nightmare!

When six o'clock came round Mr. A and Mr. P
were both exhausted. Mr. A just threw his apron over
his head and started rushing off down the street on
his long thin legs, looking neither to right nor left,

while Mr. P shooed the last customer out of the store and then sank right down on the onion crate and burst out sobbing.

He sobbed for quite a long time. When he had finished he felt a little bit better. So he mopped his eyes and blew his nose, and then he jumped up off the onion crate and rushed out of the store, not even banging the door behind him, and pattered off along the sidewalk as fast as he could go.

It was the very first time in all their lives that Mr. A and Mr. P had not walked home together. For years they had hung their two little aprons up side by side at exactly six o'clock, and at exactly two minutes past six they had taken their two hats and locked the store and strolled home side by side.

But this time Mr. A was walking much faster than Mr. P, and so Mr. P had to make his stout little legs work very hard indeed to catch up with him, but catch up he did. And as soon as Mr. A heard that little pitter-patter coming along behind him he slowed down a bit, and pretended to be looking at the landscape. So side by side, but neither looking at the other, they went along the road and across a field, until they came to a big log that was lying under a hickory tree, and there they both sat down side by side—plump!

Mr. A was still very cross, and Mr. P was still very hot and out of breath, so for a long while neither of them spoke. Then Mr. A looked round at Mr. P and gave a big sniff. And Mr. P looked at Mr. A, and he gave a sniff, too. And then they both began to wriggle their toes on the ground.

Presently Mr. P said:

"I shouldn't think you need be so mean, just because I did something to please you!"

And Mr. A said:

"Well, you didn't have to be so cross, just because I wanted to give you a s-surprise!"

"I only did it to make you laugh!" said Mr. P.

"I thought you'd be pleased and m-merry!" said Mr. A.

Then Mr. A pulled a packet of lemon drops out of his apron pocket.

"Have one," he said to Mr. P.

Mr. P took it and sucked it, and then he pulled a little packet out of *his* apron pocket, and he said to Mr. A:

"Don't you want some chewing gum?"

Half an hour later, just as the sun was setting, anyone looking out of the front window might have seen two little figures, one very tall and thin and the other very short and stout, trudging arm in arm along the sidewalk.

They were Mr. A and Mr. P, going back to their grocery store.

And from what I can hear, they have never quarreled since.

The Simpleton
and His Little Black Hen

There were three brothers left behind when the
father died. The two elder, whose names were John
and James, were as clever lads as ever ate pease with
a fork.

As for the youngest, his name was Caspar, he had
no more than enough sense to blow his potatoes when
they were hot. Well, when they came to divide things
up between themselves, John and James contrived to
share all of the good things between them. As for
Caspar, "why, the little black hen is enough for him,"
says John and James, and that was all the butter he
got from that churn.

"I'll take the little black hen to the fair," says Caspar, "and there I'll sell her and buy me some eggs.
I'll set the eggs under the minister's speckled hen, and

44]

then I'll have more chicks. Then I'll buy me more eggs and have more chicks, and then I'll buy me more eggs and have more chicks, and after that I'll be richer than Uncle Henry, who has two cows and a horse, and will marry my sweetheart into the bargain." So off he went to the fair with the black hen under his arm, as he had promised himself to do.

"There goes a goose to the plucking," says John and James, and then they turned no hairs gray by thinking any more about the case.

As for him, why, he went on and on until he came to the inn over the hill not far from the town, the host of which was no better than he should be, and that was the long and the short of it. "Where do you go with the little black hen, Caspar?" says he.

"Oh," says Caspar, "I take it to the fair to sell it and buy me some eggs. I'll set the eggs under the minister's speckled hen, and then I'll have more chicks. Then I'll buy me more eggs and have more chicks, and then I'll buy me more eggs and have more chicks, and after that I'll be richer than Uncle Henry, who has two cows and a horse, and will marry my sweetheart into the bargain."

Prut! And why should Caspar take his hen to the fair? That was what the landlord said. It was a silly thing to tramp to the river for water before the well was dry at home. Why, the landlord had a friend over

yonder who would give ten pennies to one that he
could get at the fair for his black hen. Now, had Caspar ever heard tell of the little old gentleman who
lived in the old willow tree over yonder?

No, Caspar had never heard tell of him in all of
his life. And there was no wonder in that, for no
more had anybody else, and the landlord was only up
to a bit of a trick to get the little black hen for himself.

But the landlord sucked in his lips—"*tsch*"—so!
Well, that was a pity, for the little old gentleman had
said, time and time again, that he would give a whole
bagful of gold and silver money for just such a little
black hen as the one that Caspar carried under his
arm.

Dear, dear! How Caspar's eyes did open at this, to
be sure. Off he started for the willow tree. "Here's
the little black hen," said he, "and I'll sell her for a
bagful of gold and silver money." But nobody answered him, you may be sure of that, for there was
nobody there.

"Well," says Caspar, "I'll just tie the hen to the
tree here, and you may pay me tomorrow." So he
did as he had said, and off he marched. Then came
the landlord and took the hen off home and had it for
his supper; and there was an end of that business.

An end of that business? No, no; stop a bit, for we

will not drive too fast down the hill. Listen: there
was a wicked robber who had hidden a bag of gold
and silver money in that very tree; but of that neither
Caspar nor the landlord knew any more than the
chick in the shell.

"Hi!" says Caspar, "it is the wise man who gets
along in the world." But there he was wrong for once
in his life, Tommy Pfouce tells me.

"And did you sell your hen?" says John and James,
Oh, yes; Caspar had done that.

And what had he got for it?

Oh, just a bag of gold and silver money, that was
all. He would show it to them tomorrow, for he was
to go and get it then from the old gentleman who
lived in the willow tree over yonder by the inn over
the hill.

When John and James heard that they saw as plain
as the nose on your face that Caspar had been bitten
by the *fool dog*.

But Caspar never bothered his head about that; off
he went the next day as grand as you please. Up he
marched to the willow tree, but never a soul did he
find there; for why, there was nobody.

Rap! tap! tap! He knocked upon the tree as civil
as a beggar at the kitchen door, but nobody said,
"Come in!"

"Look," says he, "we will have no dillydallying; I

want my money and I will have it," and he fetched a kick at the tree that made the bark fly. But he might as well have kicked my grandfather's bedpost for all the good he had of it. "Oh, very well!" says he, and off he marched and brought the axe that stood back of the stable door.

Hui! how the chips flew! for Caspar was bound to get to the bottom of the business. So by and by the tree lay on the ground, and there was the bag of gold and silver money that the wicked robber had hidden. "So!" says Caspar, "better late than never!" and off he marched with it.

By and by whom should he meet but John and James. Bless me, how they stared! And did Caspar get all of that money for one little black hen?

Oh, yes; that he had.

And where did he get it?

Oh! the little old man in the willow tree had paid it to him.

So, good! that was a fine thing, and it should be share and share alike among brothers; that was what John and James said, and Caspar did not say "No;" so down they all sat on the grass and began counting it out.

"This is mine," said John.

"And this is mine," said James.

"And this is mine," said John.

"And this is mine," said James.

"And where is mine?" says Caspar. But neither of the others thought of him because he was so simple.

Just then who should come along but the rogue of a landlord. "Hi! and where did you get all that?" says he.

"Oh," says Caspar, "the little old man in the willow tree paid it to me for my little black hen."

Yes, yes, the landlord knew how much of that cake to eat. He was not to have the wool pulled over his eyes so easily. See, now, he knew very well that thieving had been done, and he would have them all up before the master mayor for it. So the upshot of the matter was that they had to take him in to share with them.

"This is mine," says the landlord.

"And this is mine," says John.

"And this is mine," says James.

"And where do I come in?" says poor Caspar. But nobody thought of him because he was so simple.

Just then came along a company of soldiers— tramp! tramp! tramp!—and there they found them all sharing the money between them, except Caspar.

"Hi!" says the captain, "here are a lot of thieves, and no mistake!" and off he marched them to the king's house, which was finer than any in our town, and as big as a church into the bargain.

And how had they come by all that money? that was what the king would like to know.

As for the three rogues, they sang a different tune now than they had whistled before.

"It's none of mine, it's his," said the landlord, and he pointed to John.

"It's none of mine, it's his," said John, and he pointed to James.

"It's none of mine, it's his," said James, and he pointed to Caspar.

"And how did you get it?" says the king.

"Oh!" says Caspar, "the little old man in the willow tree gave it to me for my little black hen;" and he told the whole story without missing a single grain.

Beside the king sat the princess, who was so serious and solemn that she had never laughed once in all her life. So the king had said, time and time again, that whoever should make her laugh should have her for his wife. Now, when she heard Caspar's story, and how he came in behind all the rest, so that he always had the pinching, like the tail of our cat in the crack of the door, she laughed like everything, for she could not help it. So there was the fat in the fire, for Caspar was not much to look at, and that was the truth. Dear, dear, what a stew the king was in, for he had no notion for Caspar as a son-in-law. So he began to think about striking a bargain. "Come," says he to

Caspar, "how much will you take to give up the princess instead of marrying her?"

Well, Caspar did not know how much a princess was worth. So he scratched his head and scratched his head, and by and by he said that he would be willing to take ten dollars and let the princess go.

At this the king boiled over into a mighty fume, like water into the fire. What! did Caspar think that ten dollars was a fit price for a princess!

Oh, Caspar had never done any business of this kind before. He had a sweetheart of his own at home, and if ten dollars was too much for the princess he would be willing to take five.

Sakes alive! what a rage the king was in! Why, I would not have stood in Caspar's shoes just then—no, not for a hundred dollars. The king would have had him whipped right away, only just then he had some other business on hand. So he paid Caspar his five dollars, and told him that if he would come back the next day he should have all that his back could carry —meaning a whipping.

As for Caspar and his brothers and the rogue of a landlord, they thought that the king was talking about dollars. So when they had left the king's house and had come out into the road again, the three rogues began to talk as smooth and as soft as though their words were buttered.

See, now, what did Caspar want with all that the king had promised him; that was what they said. If he would let them have it, they would give him all of their share of the money he had found in the willow tree.

"Ah, yes," says Caspar, "I am willing to do that. For," says he to himself, "an apple in the pocket is worth three on the tree." And there he was right for once in his life.

Well, the next day back they all tramped to the king's house again to get what had been promised to Caspar.

So! Caspar had come back for the rest, had he?

Oh, yes, he had come back again; but the lord king must know that he had sold all that had been promised to him to these three lads for their share of the money he had found in the willow tree over yonder.

"Yes," says the landlord, "one part of what has been promised is mine."

"And one part of it is mine," says John.

"Stop a bit, brother," says James; "remember, one part of it is mine too."

At this the king could not help laughing, and that broke the back of his anger.

First of all he sent the landlord for his share, and if his back did not smart after he had it, why, it was not the fault of those who gave it to him. By and by he came back again, but he said nothing to the others of what had been given to him; but all the same he grinned as though he had been eating sour gooseberries. Then John went, and last of all James, and what they got satisfied them, I can tell you.

After that the king told Caspar that he might go into the other room and fill his pockets with money for what he had given up to the others; so he had the cool end of that bargain, and did not burn his fingers after all.

But the three rogues were not satisfied with this No, indeed! Caspar should have his share of the smarting, see if he shouldn't! So back they went to the king's house one fine day, and said Caspar had been talking about the lord king, and had said that he was no better than an old hunks. At this the king was awfully angry. And so off he sent the others to fetch Caspar along so that he might settle the score with him.

When the three came home, there was Caspar lying on a bench in the sun, for he could take the world easy now, because he was so rich.

"Come along, Caspar," said they, "the king wants to see you over at his house yonder."

Yes, yes, but there was too much hurrying in this business, for it was over-quick cooking that burned the broth. If Caspar was to go to the king's house he would go in fitting style, so they would just have to wait till he found a horse, for he was not going to jog it afoot; that was what Caspar said.

"Yes," says the landlord, "but sooner than you should lose time in the waiting, I will lend you my fine dapple-gray."

But where was the bridle to come from? Caspar would have them know that he was not going to ride a horse to the king's house without a good bridle over the nag's ears.

Oh, John would lend him the new bridle that he bought in the town last week; so that was soon settled.

But how about the saddle? That was what Caspar wanted to know—yes, how about the saddle? Did they think that he was going to ride up to the king's house with his heels thumping against the horse's ribs as though he were no better than a plowman?

Oh, James would lend him a saddle if that was all he wanted.

So off they went, all four of them, to the king's house.

There was the king, walking up and down, and fussing and fuming with anger till he was all of a heat.

"See, now," says he, as soon as he saw Caspar, "what did you call me an old hunks for?"

"I didn't call you an old hunks," said Caspar.

"Yes, you did," said the king.

"No, I didn't," said Caspar.

"Yes, you did," said the king, "for these three lads told me so."

"Prut!" said Caspar, "who would believe what they say? Why, they would just as lief tell you that this horse and saddle and bridle belong to them."

"And so they do!" bawled the three rogues.

"See there, now," said Caspar.

The king scratched his head, for here was a tangled knot, for certain. "Yes, yes," said he, "these fellows are fooling either Caspar or me, and we are both in the same tub, for the matter of that. Take them away and whip them!" So it was done as he said, and that was all that they got for their trouble.

Wit and Luck are not always hatched in the same nest, says Tommy Pfouce, and maybe he is right about it, for Caspar married his sweetheart, and if she did not keep his money for him, and himself out of trouble, she would not have been worth speaking of, and I, for one, would never have told this story.

Conal and Donal and Taig

Once there were three brothers named Conal, Donal
and Taig, and they fell out regarding which of them
owned a field of land. One of them had as good a
claim to it as the other, and the claims of all of them
were so equal that none of the judges, whomsoever
they went before, could decide in favor of one more
than the other.

At length they went to one judge who was very
wise indeed and had a great name, and every one of
them stated his case to him.

He sat on the bench, and heard Conal's case and

Donal's case and Taig's case all through, with very great patience. When the three of them had finished, he said he would take a day and a night to think it all over, and on the day after, when they were all called into court again, the Judge said that he had weighed the evidence on all sides, with all the deliberation it was possible to give it, and he decided that one of them hadn't the shadow of a shade of a claim more than the others, so that he found himself facing the greatest puzzle he had ever faced in his life.

"But," says he, "no puzzle puzzles me long. I'll very soon decide which of you will get the field. You seem to me to be three pretty lazy-looking fellows, and I'll give the field to whichever of the three of you is the laziest."

"Well, at that rate," says Conal, "it's me gets the field, for I'm the laziest man of the lot."

"How lazy are you?" says the Judge.

"Well," said Conal, "if I were lying in the middle of the road, and there was a regiment of troopers come galloping down it, I'd sooner let them ride over me than take the bother of getting up and going to the one side."

"Well, well," says the Judge, says he, "you are a lazy man surely, and I doubt if Donal or Taig can be as lazy as that."

"Oh, faith," says Donal, "I'm just every bit as lazy."

"Are you?" says the Judge. "How lazy are you?"

"Well," said Donal, "if I was sitting right close to a big fire, and you piled on it all the turf in a townland and all the wood in a barony, sooner than have to move I'd sit there till the boiling marrow would run out of my bones."

"Well," says the Judge, "you're a pretty lazy man, Donal, and I doubt if Taig is as lazy as either of you."

"Indeed, then," says Taig, "I'm every bit as lazy."

"How can that be?" says the Judge.

"Well," says Taig, "if I was lying on the broad of my back in the middle of the floor and looking up at the rafters, and if soot drops were falling as thick as hailstones from the rafters into my open eyes, I would let them drop there for the length of the lee-long day sooner than take the bother of closing the eyes."

"Well," says the Judge, "that's very wonderful entirely, and," says he, "I'm in as great a quandary as before, for I see you are the three laziest men that ever were known since the world began, and which of you is the laziest it certainly beats me to say. But I'll tell you what I'll do," says the Judge. "I'll give the field to the oldest man of you."

"Then," says Conal, "it's me gets the field."

"How is that?" says the Judge; "how old are you?"

"Well, I'm that old," says Conal, "that when I was twenty-one years of age I got a shipload of awls and never lost nor broke one of them, and I wore out the last of them yesterday mending my shoes."

"Well, well," says the Judge, says he, "you're surely an old man, and I doubt very much that Donal and Taig can catch up to you."

"Can't I?" says Donal. "Take care of that."

"Why," said the Judge, "how old are you?"

"When I was twenty-one years of age," says Donal, "I got a shipload of needles, and yesterday I wore out the last of them mending my clothes."

"Well, well, well," says the Judge, says he, "you're two very, very old men, to be sure, and I'm afraid poor Taig is out of his chance anyhow."

"Take care of that," says Taig.

"Why," said the Judge, "how old are you, Taig?"

Says Taig, "When I was twenty-one years of age I got a shipload of razors, and yesterday I had the last of them worn to a stump shaving myself."

"Well," says the Judge, says he, "I've often heard tell of old men," he says, "but anything as old as what you are never was known since Methusalem's cat died. The like of your ages," he says, "I never heard tell of, and which of you is the oldest, that surely beats me to decide, and I'm in a quandary again. But

I'll tell you what I'll do," says the Judge, says he, "I'll give the field to whichever of you minds (re-members) the longest."

"Well, if that's it," says Conal, "it's me gets the field, for I mind the time when if a man tramped on a cat he usen't to give it a kick to console it."

"Well, well, well," says the Judge, "that must be a long mind entirely; and I'm afraid, Conal, you have the field."

"Not so quick," says Donal, says he, "for I mind the time when a woman wouldn't speak an ill word of her best friend."

"Well, well, well," says the Judge, "your memory, Donal, must certainly be a very wonderful one, if you can mind that time. Taig," says the Judge, says he, "I'm afraid your memory can't compare with Conal's and Donal's."

"Can't it?" says Taig, says he. "Take care of that, for I mind the time when you wouldn't find nine liars in a crowd of ten men."

"Oh, oh, oh!" says the Judge, says he, "that memory of yours, Taig, must be a wonderful one." Says he: "Such memories as you three men have were never known before, and which of you has the greatest memory it beats me to say. But I'll tell you what I'll do now," says he; "I'll give the field to whichever of you has the keenest sight."

"Then," says Conal, says he, "it's me gets the field; because," says he, "if there was a fly perched on the top of yon mountain, ten miles away, I could tell you every time he blinked."

"You have wonderful sight, Conal," says the Judge, says he, "and I'm afraid you've got the field."

"Take care," says Donal, says he, "but I've got as good. For I could tell you whether it was a mote in his eye that made him blink or not."

"Ah, ha, ha!" says the Judge, says he. "This is wonderful sight surely. Taig," says he, "I pity you, for you have no chance for the field now."

"Have I not?" says Taig. "I could tell you from here whether that fly was in good health or not by counting his heart beats."

"Well, well, well," says the Judge, says he, "I'm in as great a quandary as ever. You are three of the most wonderful men that ever I met, and no mistake. But I'll tell you what I'll do," says he; "I'll give the field to the supplest man of you."

"Thank you," says Conal. "Then the field is mine."

"Why so?" says the Judge.

"Because," says Conal, says he, "if you filled that field with hares, and put a dog in the middle of them, and then tied one of my legs up my back, I would not let one of the hares get out."

"Then, Conal," says the Judge, says he, "I think the field is yours."

"By the leave of your judgeship, not yet," says Donal.

"Why, Donal," says the Judge, says he, "surely you are not as supple as that?"

"Am I not?" says Donal. "Do you see that old castle over there without door, or window, or roof in it, and the wind blowing in and out through it like an iron gate?"

"I do," says the Judge. "What about that?"

"Well," says Donal, says he, "if on the stormiest day of the year you had that castle filled with feathers, I would not let a feather be lost, or go ten yards from the castle until I had caught and put it in again."

"Well, surely," says the Judge, says he, "you are a supple man, Donal, and no mistake. Taig," says he, "there's no chance for you now."

"Don't be too sure," says Taig, says he.

"Why," says the Judge, "you couldn't surely do anything to equal these things, Taig?"

Says Taig, says he: "I can shoe the swiftest race horse in the land when he is galloping at his topmost speed, by driving a nail everytime he lifts his foot."

"Well, well, well," says the Judge, says he, "surely you are the three most wonderful men that ever I did

meet. The likes of you never was known before, and
I suppose the likes of you never will be on the earth
again. There is only one other trial," says he, "and if
this doesn't decide, I'll have to give it up. I'll give
the field," says he, "to the cleverest man amongst
you."

"Then," says Conal, says he, "you may as well give
it to me at once."

"Why? Are you that clever, Conal?" says the Judge,
says he.

"I am that clever," says Conal. "I am that clever,
that I would make a skin-fit suit of clothes for a man
without any more measurement than to tell me the
color of his hair."

"Then, boys," says the Judge, says he, "I think the
case is decided."

"Not so quick, my friend," says Donal, "not so
quick."

"Why, Donal," says the Judge, says he, "you are
surely not cleverer than that?"

"Am I not?" says Donal.

"Why," says the Judge, says he, "what can you do,
Donal?"

"Why," says Donal, says he, "I would make a skin-
fit suit for a man and give me no more measurement
than let me hear him cough."

"Well, well, well," says the Judge, says he, "the

cleverness of you two boys beats all I ever heard of. Taig," says he, "poor Taig, whatever chance either of these two may have for the field, I'm very, very sorry for you, for you have no chance."

"Don't be so very sure of that," says Taig, says he.

"Why," says the Judge, says he, "surely, Taig, you can't be as clever as either of them. How clever are you, Taig?"

"Well," says Taig, says he, "if I was a judge, and too stupid to decide a case that came up before me, I'd be that clever that I'd look wise and give some decision."

"Taig," says the Judge, says he, "I've gone into this case and deliberated upon it, and by all the laws of right and justice, I find and decide that you get the field."

The Drawbridge

"What about going on a trip?" I said.

"Where?" Lee asked. She wouldn't say yes to just *any* trip.

"Oh, I don't know, myself," I said. "I was thinking of Alaska, or Boston, or around the block."

"Oh, Mother, not *really* around the block," Elinor said. "That's not a trip."

"It depends on who's going round it, I suppose," I said. "*You* always trip it. I can't keep up with you. No, I don't really mean around the block. I was thinking of just going somewhere to wear out the car so we would have to afford to buy a new one. We could keep going until it dropped to pieces. That might mean we'd get as far as Mexico City, but it might mean we'd only—"

"Get as far as Pittsfield?" Lee asked.

"That's right," I said. "Or we might even stick on a hill half way. Shall we try?"

"Of course," they said together. So we tried.

But there were lots of difficulties to begin with. Elinor and Lee said they must take eighteen dolls apiece (not counting three hundred paper-dolls), and all their crayons (even the broken ones), and the good victrola (with chiefly the Gilbert and Sullivan records). And I said I must take one hundred and fifty most important books and some cold cream. Then there was gum and candy (*not* licorice), and sun glasses, and playing cards, and the tame giraffe, and a frying pan and can opener in case we ran out of gas in the desert and no one came along.

Then Elinor and Lee *suddenly* said they had to take their three cousins (Prescott, Jackie, and Robin), and the three cousins said they had to take their three dogs. We were rather packed in, and quite heavy.

We were so heavy we had four flat tires before I could manage to back out of the garage. They were very old tires. I suppose that was why. And they all blew out at once, which made such a noise the gas company called up to ask if it was the gas stove exploding, and the police department called up to ask who we thought we were shooting at. We said it was purely accidental, just our cannon had gone off before we were quite ready. Then we hung up, rather quickly I'm afraid, because we couldn't keep a straight face.

We ordered four new tires out of a big catalogue and sat in the garage for two weeks until they came. But it was fun sitting there because Lee and Robin began laughing when the gas company called up and simply couldn't stop. It was a two-week laugh. But the laugh was on us when the tires came and we remembered we had lost the jack and the wrench in Mexico last year. So we drove to a service station on the flat tires and let them do the changing. Elinor said we could have done that in the first place and saved two weeks. I suppose we could have only we didn't think of it.

When we finally started it was snowing in New England, hurricaning in Florida, sandstorming in Kansas, and earthquaking in California. The newspapers said so. We had to take care not to go there at least. We asked a policeman about it at the next corner, and we *thought* he said, "Keep to the left." The dogs were barking at the time, the cousins were singing, Elinor and Lee were arguing, and the tame giraffe had stopped being tame and was making faces at people out the back window (I could see him in the mirror). So no wonder I *thought* the policeman said, "Keep to the left." Anyway we kept to the left and found ourselves in a pickle. There was mud up to the hubs, stones under the mud, rain coming down in buckets, lots of buzzards flying around, lots of Spanish moss hanging around, and a very wide river we couldn't get across.

"This must be Mississippi," Lee said.

"Mississippi or Mrs. Anybody," I said, "whichever it is, it's awful, even with new tires." And just then one of the fenders flew off and the fan belt snapped.

"We're going to pieces quite rapidly," Prescott remarked. "Do you think we'll make South America tonight?"

"Your sense of geography is extremely poor," I said, "and we'll be lucky if we cross this river at all. Oh, here's a bridge. That's *some*thing."

It certainly turned out to *be* something. It was a drawbridge, the longest drawbridge we had ever seen in all our travels, and it began to draw before we had quite reached the middle. We were hoisted up and up. We all held onto the car hard, hoping the car would take the hint and hold onto the bridge hard. But you can't teach an old car new tricks. We had been going nearly twenty miles an hour forward. Now we went at least fifty-five miles an hour backward. It was just like a roller-coaster, only the wrong way round. Jackie said we would be dizzy-sick if we didn't turn our seats around, too, the way you can in trains. But the dogs were so tangled up with the seats, we couldn't manage. The dogs helped a little, though, by howling so much I didn't need to use the horn. Anyone could have heard us coming or going.

When we slowed down at last, I found I couldn't shut off the motor. The ignition was jammed (Prescott said something scientific about it I couldn't understand), so before we could say Jack Robinson we were climbing that bridge again. It was miserable. I thought surely we would go right over the top edge. But the car didn't have the strength to make it. We climbed up hundreds of feet into the air on smooth asphalt, and then came *shooting* down backward again. We kept doing it—up and down, up and down, like a see-saw. We saw the bridge man running back and forth waving his arms at us to stop it. Prescott waved back. We were too far away, and going too fast to hear what he was saying. He looked like Charlie Chaplin being excited in a silent movie.

We wanted to stop in the worst way. This was wearing the car out much faster than was safe. We were squeaking all over. And pieces of us were coming off and rattling down like hail. Then a worse thing happened. We went up too fast and the front wheels caught over the top edge. We hung there.

"This is precarious," I said.

"What's precarious mean?" Lee asked from an upside-down-cake position.

"Risky," I said. "Don't ask questions when things are as precarious as this."

The bridge man thought it was precarious, too. He completely lost his head when he saw us hanging on by the skin of our teeth like this and began lowering the drawbridge. That was a fatal mistake. It caught the boat just half through the opening and drove the masts right down through the bottom, like one of those nursery pegs-and-hammer toys—you know the kind I mean. Elinor said it was the easiest and quickest way to make the boat look upside down. But the Captain was quite angry. He and Jackie had a strong argument about it. But Lee said, "Oh, stop quarreling. Nobody is 'xactly to blame. This is just an accident."

I agreed with her that it was an accident in more ways than one. Because when the bridge came down it caught our front wheels between the two sections and pinched them off as neat as a pin. Elinor said it was a clean cut anyway. But I saw that our trip was going to end right here in the middle of a drawbridge. So I asked the children to help make the best of a hard time. We decided to give the Captain's children all of the candy and gum that was left over in order to make the Captain feel better about the masts. And we gave Prescott's *Mechano* set to the bridge man because he was really mechanical-minded, even

if he *had* made two or three mistakes that afternoon.
We gave the rest of the car to a farmer who lived along
the river. He quickly attached some handles to the
front and made a wheelbarrow. He had needed a
wheelbarrow for some time.

Robin said, "Well, I guess the drawbridge isn't
damaged very much."

"No," I said, "the drawbridge looks as well as ever.
That's lucky."

"But *how* are we going to get home?" Lee asked.

"In the new car, of course," I said. "What did you
expect?"

Baby Rainstorm

One spring, a good many years back, Paul Bunyan had a logging camp on the headwaters of the River That Ran Sidewise. He'd had a profitable winter and the landings were jammed full of logs decked up and waiting for the spring floods to float them down to the mills.

74]

Finally, the weather turned warm and the snow started to melt. A few more days and the big drive would be under way. Then one morning the men woke up to find it raining! Now rain is not so unusual at that time of year, but this was no ordinary rain. No siree, Bob. For where the ordinary rain comes down, this came up. All over the camp, and as far as any one could see, streams of big raindrops were squirting up out of the ground, sailing straight up in the air and disappearing into the clouds overhead!

And with it came trouble. For, as any one knows, almost all the rain in this country comes down, so of course we build our houses to take care of that kind of rain, seldom giving the other kind a thought. And that was the case in Ol' Paul's camp. The buildings all had tight roofs that water wouldn't come through, but the floors, on the other hand, were made with wide cracks so that water and mud tracked in by the lumberjacks would run through to the ground below.

But now, with the rain coming up, the floors leaked like sieves and the water gathered on the ceilings and couldn't leak out. By the time the men woke up there was four feet of water on the under side of the ceiling of every bunkhouse in camp, and it was getting deeper every minute. The men as they got up had to duck their heads to keep from bumping into the water.

One of the loggers hotfooted it over to Paul's office to tell him about it.

"Paul!" he hollered when he could get his breath. "The rain is a-comin' straight up this morning!"

"Yuh mean it's a-clabberin' up to rain, don't yuh?" Paul asked, as he hunted under his bunk for his socks. "Why the Sam Hill don't yuh learn to say what yuh mean?"

"Nossir!" the lumberjack insisted. "I meant jest what I said, that the rain is a-comin' straight up outta the ground and yuh kin take a look fer yerself!"

Ol' Paul finally discovered that he already had his socks on because he'd never taken them off when he went to bed, so he put on his boots and stomped over to the window to see what was what. At first he couldn't believe his eyes, so he put the window up to get a better look, and still he didn't believe what he saw. He tried looking out of first one eye and then the other; then he got out his specs, which he most usually didn't wear except when there was no one around, and clamped them on his nose and went outside to have a good close look. But any way he looked at it, the rain was sure enough coming straight up.

So Ol' Paul and the lumberjack sat down to think about it.

After a while the lumberjack spoke up. "Paul," says he, "a feller is kinda prepared fer ordinary rain, fer all his clothes are made to take care of it, if yuh ever noticed."

"How do yuh figger that?" Paul wanted to know, not too enthusiastically.

"Why a feller's hat sticks out so the rain won't run down his collar, much. And his coat overlaps his britches, and his britches overlaps his boots. It's sorta like he was shingled, if yuh see what I mean."

"Yeah," said Paul. "So where does that leave us?"

"Well, when the rain comes up, instead of down, it falls straight up his britches legs, straight up under his coat, and straight up his sleeves! It's mighty, mighty uncomfortable. Wonder, now, if it wouldn't be possible to sorta shingle a feller backwards, like."

And then they sat and thought some more, since the big bear skin in the middle of Paul's floor kept the rain from hitting them as it came up.

Meanwhile, the lumberjacks over in the bunkhouses, and the stable bucks and the bull cooks and the mess hall flunkeys were all in a very bad humor. The cooks were in a bad humor, too, but camp cooks are almost always that way so nobody noticed any particular difference.

After a while a delegation came to Ol' Paul and told him that he'd better do something about this business pretty soon or they'd all quit and go to work for Sowbelly Burke, his rival.

Ol' Paul assured them that he'd get to the bottom of the mystery as soon as possible, but pointed out to them that it would take time, since nothing like it had ever happened before. That being the case there was of course nothing written in the books about how to deal with it. So he'd have to figure it all out by himself.

Besides, he told them, think of the stories you can tell in the towns this summer, about how you got your drive out in spite of the rain that fell straight up!

But they were still mad and going to quit, so he saw he'd have to take measures pretty quick.

After quite a spell of unusually heavy thinking, he called for Johnnie Inkslinger to quick make out an order to his favorite mail-order house for enough bumbershoots to make two apiece for all the men in camp.

"Bumbershoots?" Johnnie asked. "What's bumbershoots?"

"Why the things folks hold up over their heads when it's raining," says Paul. "I've seen pitchers of them in the catalogues many's the time."

"What you mean is Umbrellas," says Johnnie, who comes from up Boston way and always talks sort of special. "And besides," says he, "they will do no good in this emergency, because they are made for rain

that falls down and this rain is indubitably coming
straight up instead."

"You go on and do like I say," says Paul. "I cal'late
to figger out a way to use 'em by the time I get 'em.
Tell 'em this is a hustle up order."

A couple days later the bumbershoots came, two
for every man jack in camp, and you should have
heard the lumberjacks roar. No self-respecting lumberjack had ever been known to carry one of the sissy
things and they weren't going to start it now. They
might be all right for city dudes, but not for regular
he-lumberjacks! No, sir! They'd quit first.

Ol' Paul went on helping Ole open the boxes and
told the lumberjacks just to keep their shirts on a
minute till they saw what he had in mind.

As fast as the bumbershoots were unpacked, the
Little Chore boy opened them up an' Ol' Paul took
his jackknife and cut the handles off short inside and
fastened on a couple of snowshoe loops, instead.
When he had them all fixed up he had Johnnie call
the roll. As each logger came up Paul handed him a
couple of the remodeled bumbershoots and told him
to slip his feet into the loops. The first men were a
mite shy about the business, but after they had put
them on and straddled off, as if they were wearing
snowshoes, they found that the bumbershoots did

keep the rain from coming up their pants legs. And
from then on the men pushed and hollered for the
line ahead to hurry up so they could get theirs.

"See there," says Ol' Paul, "I guess I knowed what
I was doing. I don't reckon there is anything sissy
about wearing bumbershoots on your feet. And, any-
ways, we'll call 'em bumbershoes from now on, just
to be sure!"

The men all cheered again, and decided not to quit
camp after all.

The next morning a friendly Indian, Chief Rink-
tumdiddy by name, came tearing in to camp wanting
to see Paul. He told Ol' Paul that he and another
Indian were out hunting the day before and they
camped by the mouth of a cave out on the prairie a
way. After they'd eaten their supper they decided to
explore this cave, so they took along some pine knots
for torches, and started out. They went back through
the narrow twisting passages for about a half a mile,
as near as they could judge, when all of a sudden they
heard the awfullest noise they'd ever laid an ear next
to. They didn't stop to argue, but tore out of there
as fast as they could. They figured that by going in
there they had made the Great Spirit mad, and that
he it was they heard hollering. So now this Indian
wanted Paul to see if he could talk the Great Spirit
out of his mad.

Ol' Paul was plumb curious, but from what the Chief told him, he knew the cave was too small for him to get into, and he hadn't Babe along to burrow for him, so he sat still and thought for a spell. Finally, he allowed as how maybe two men listening together could listen far enough back to hear the noise from the mouth of the cave. That sounded like a good idea, but the Indian was plumb scared to go back, so Paul called Chris Crosshaul to go along instead.

The cave wasn't hard to find, and when they got there they both listened as hard as they could and, sure enough, they just about heard the noise. But when they tried listening separately they couldn't hear a sound. (It's a well known fact that two men listening together can hear twice as far as one man listening alone.)

For a while Paul listened to the rumpus he could hear going on back in the cave, and a very curious sound it was, too. It was sort of mixed up with whimpering and whining like a lost puppy, and dribbling, splashing sounds, and a sort of pattering; and, now and again, a hollow booming such as lightning might make if shut up in a cellar.

After a spell of especially hard listening that left them both red in the face and out of breath, Paul turned to Chris and said, "Chris, thet's nuthing in the wide world but a baby rainstorm thet's got himself lost back in this here cave, and now he's bellering fer his maw!"

"Yuh don't say," says Chris, doubtful like.

"Yessir!" says Paul, "and by looking at my pocket compass I've discovered thet the noise is a-coming from right under our lumbercamp! The way I figger it, thet little feller got separated from the rest of the herd and got in here by mistake awhile back. Now, he's lost and scared. You jest heerd him whimpering and thundering his heart out back in there. Chances are he's got all upset in the dark there and is raining straight up instead of down and don't know it. We gotta get him outta there."

"Yeah?" says Chris Crosshaul. "It sounds reasonable, but how the Sam Hill we gonna git him out?"

"Well, the way I see it," says Ol' Paul, when they had their pipes going good, "the only way to get thet critter outta there is to call him out. It's a cinch we can't drag him out because there is no way to catch hold of a critter like that. And nobody ever had any luck trying to chase a rainstorm anywheres thet I ever heard tell about."

"Reckon you're right thet fur, Paul," says Chris, "but I never hear tell of any one that can call a rainstorm, neither."

"That's the beauty of the whole thing," says **Paul**. "We'll be the first ones to ever do such a thing."

"Jest how do yuh figger to go about it?" Chris wants to know. "Yuh don't mean yuh kin holler like rainstorms, do yuh?"

"Not right now, I can't," says Paul. "But I figger I kin soon learn how. Yuh see, I know a feller in Kansas City thet will rent yuh all kinds of disguises. I'll git him to disguise me up to look like a rainstorm, then I'll go out and live with a tribe of 'em and learn their language. Should be simple enough, shouldn't it?"

And that's just what he did. He got himself all dressed up in a rainstorm suit till you wouldn't have known him. Then he went out into Iowa where most of the rainstorms summered. He fell in with a big tribe of them, and his disguise was so perfect that they just figured he was a strange rainstorm, maybe blown up from Texas way, and they invited him to stay with them as long as he liked.

He had a mighty fine time all summer, helping the rainstorms to soak open-air political meetings, and the like, although probably he took an unfair advantage at times. He always managed to get the rainstorms to rain on people he didn't want elected, and kept them away from the rallies of people he liked.

But, anyway, late in the summer he came back, and just to show off he was always throwing rainstorm words into his talk, till the lumberjacks scarcely knew what he was talking about. Then one day he went over to the mouth of the cave where the rainstorm was. Getting down on his hands and knees, he put his face up close to the entrance to the cave and imitated the cry a mother rainstorm makes when she is calling her young ones.

As soon as he did that, the noise and thundering and blubbering inside the cave stopped at once. There wasn't a sound to be heard, and the rain, for the first time all summer, stopped coming up around camp.

"See thet," says Paul, with a big grin. And then he hollered the rainstorm holler again, and that little rainstorm came tearing out of the cave as if he'd been sent for and couldn't come. He was just a little fellow compared to what some rainstorms are, and a mite puny-looking from being shut in the dark for so long. He jumped into Ol' Paul's arms and licked his face and rained all over him like an excited puppy dog.

Ol' Paul petted him and talked to him soothingly, till he quieted down, then sent him off down to Iowa where the rest of the rainstorms are. The last we saw of him he was just a little cloud over in the next county, and plumb decked out with rainbows, he was so tickled.

The Laughing Prince

There was once a farmer who had three sons and one little daughter. The eldest son was a studious boy who learned so much out of books that the farmer said:

"We must send Mihailo to school and make a priest of him."

The second boy was a trader. Whatever you had he

would get it from you by offering you something else for it. And always what he gave you was worth less than what you gave him.

"Jakov will make a fine peddler," the farmer said. "He's industrious and sharp and some day he will probably be a rich man."

But Stefan, the farmer's youngest son, had no special talent and because he didn't spend all his time with his nose in a book and because he never made the best of a bargain his brothers scorned him. Militza, his little sister, loved him dearly for he was kind and jolly and in the evening he was always ready to tell her stories and play with her. But the farmer, of course, listened to the older brothers.

"I don't know about poor Stefan," he used to say. "He's a good boy but he talks nonsense. I suppose he'll have to stay on the farm and work."

Now the truth is the farm was a fine place for Stefan for he was strong and lusty and he liked to plow and harvest and he had a wonderful way with the animals. He talked to them as if they were human beings and the horses all whinnied when he came near, and the cows rubbed their soft noses against his shoulder, and as for the pigs—they loved him so much that whenever they saw him they used to run squealing between his legs.

"Stefan is nothing but a farmer!" Mihailo used to

say as though being a farmer was something to be ashamed of.

And Jakov said, "If the village people could see the pigs following him about, how they'd laugh at him! I hope when I go to the village to live he won't be visiting me all the time!"

Another thing the older brothers couldn't understand about Stefan was why he was always laughing and joking. He did the work of two men but whether he was working or resting you could always hear him cracking his merry jokes and laughing his jolly laugh.

"I think he's foolish!" Mihailo said.

Jakov hoped that the village people wouldn't hear about his carryings on.

"They'd laugh at him," he said, "and they'd laugh at us, too, because we're his brothers."

But Stefan didn't care. The more they frowned at him, the louder he laughed, and in spite of their dark looks he kept on cracking his merry jokes and talking nonsense. And every evening after supper his little sister, Militza, clapped her hands and cried:

"Now, Stefan, tell me a story! Tell me a story!"

"Father," Milhailo would say, "you ought to make him keep quiet! He's foolish and all he does is fill Militza's head with nonsense!"

This always made Militza very indignant and she would stamp her little foot and say, "He isn't foolish! He knows more than any one! And he can do more things than any one else and he's the handsomest brother in the world!"

You see Militza loved Stefan dearly and when you love a person of course you think that person is wonderful. But the father supposed that Mihailo must be right for Mihailo studied in books. So he shook his head and sighed every time he thought of Stefan.

Now the kingdom in which the three brothers lived was ruled over by a great Tsar who had an only daughter. In disappointment that he had no son, the Tsar was having his daughter brought up as though she were a boy. He sent all over the world for tutors and teachers and had the poor girl taught statecraft and law and philosophy and all the other things that the heir to the throne ought to know.

The Princess because she was an obedient girl and because she loved her father tried to spend all her time in study. But the dry old scholars whom the Tsar employed as teachers were not amusing companions for a young girl and the first lady-in-waiting who was in constant attendance was scarcely any better for she, too, was old and thin and very prim.

If the poor Princess between her geography lesson and her arithmetic lesson would peep for a moment into a mirror, the first lady-in-waiting would tap her arm reprovingly and say, "My dear, vanity is not becoming in a princess!"

One day the little Princess lost her temper and answered sharply:

"But I'm a girl even if I am a princess and I love to look in mirrors and I love to make myself pretty and I'd love to go to a ball every night of my life and dance with handsome young men!"

"You talk like the daughter of a farmer!" the first lady-in-waiting said.

Then the Princess, because she lost her temper still further, said something she should not have said.

"I wish I were the daughter of a farmer!" she declared. "Then I would wear pretty ribbons and go dancing and the boys would come courting me! As it is I have to spend all my time with funny old men and silly old women!"

Now even if her tutors and teachers were funny looking old men, even if the first lady-in-waiting was a silly old woman, the Princess should not have said so. It hurt the feelings of the first lady-in-waiting and made her angry and she ran off to the Tsar at once and complained most bitterly.

"Is this my reward after all my years of loving service to your daughter?" she asked. "It is true that I've grown old and thin, looking after her manners and now she calls me a silly old woman! And all the learned wise men and scholars that you have gathered from the far corners of the earth—she points her finger at them and calls them funny old men!"

The fact is they were funny looking, most of them, but yet the first lady-in-waiting was right: the Princess should not have said so.

"And think of her ingratitude to yourself, O Tsar!" the first lady-in-waiting continued. "You plan to make her the heir to your throne and yet she says she wishes she were a farmer's daughter so that she could deck herself out in ribbons and have the boys come courting her! A nice thing for a princess to say!"

The Tsar when he heard this fell into an awful rage. (The truth is whatever temper the Princess had she inherited direct from her father.)

"Wow! Wow!" he roared, just that way. "Send the princess to me at once. I'll soon have her singing another tune!"

So the first lady-in-waiting sent the Princess to her father and as soon as he saw her he began roaring again and saying, "Wow! Wow! What do you mean— funny old men and silly old women?"

Now whenever the Tsar began roaring and saying, "Wow! Wow!" the Princess always stiffened, and instead of being the sweet and obedient daughter she usually was she became obstinate. Her pretty eyes would flash and her soft pretty face would harden and people would whisper, "Mercy on us, how much she looks like her father!"

"That's just what I mean!" the Princess said. "They're a lot of funny old men and silly old women and I'm tired of them! I want to be amused! I want to laugh!"

"Wow! Wow! Wow!" roared the Tsar. "A fine princess you are! Go straight back to the schoolroom and behave yourself!"

So the little Princess marched out of the throne room holding her head very high and looking so much like the Tsar that the first lady-in-waiting was positively frightened.

The Princess went back to the schoolroom but she did not behave herself. She was really very naughty. When the poor man who knew more than anybody in the world about the influence of the stars upon the destinies of nations came to give her a lesson, she threw his book out the window. When the super-annuated old general who was teaching her military maneuvers offered her a diagram on which the enemy was represented by a series of black dots and our soldiers by a series of red dots, she took the paper and tore it in two. And worst of all when the old scholar who was teaching her Turkish—for a princess must be able to speak all languages—dropped his horn

spectacles on the floor, she deliberately stepped on them and broke them.

When the Tsar heard all these things he just *wow-wowed* something terrible.

"Lock that young woman in her chamber!" he ordered. "Feed her on bread and water until she's ready to apologize!"

But the Princess, far from being frightened by this treatment, calmly announced, "I won't eat even your old bread and water until you send me some one who will make me laugh!"

Now this frightened the Tsar because he knew how obstinate the Princess could be on occasions. (He ought to know, too, for the Princess had that streak of obstinacy direct from himself.)

"This will never do!" he said.

He hurried to the Princess's chamber. He found her in bed with her pretty hair spread out on the pillow like a golden fan.

"My dear," the Tsar said, "I was joking. You don't have to eat only bread and water. You may have anything you want."

"Thank you," the Princess said, "but I'll never eat another bite of anything until you send me some one who will make me laugh. I'm tired of living in this gloomy old castle with a lot of old men and old women who do nothing but instruct me and with a father who always loses his temper and says, 'Wow! Wow!' "

"But it's a beautiful castle!" the poor Tsar said. "And I'm sure we're all doing our very best to educate you!"

"But I want to be amused as well as educated!" the little Princess said. And then, because she felt she was going to cry, she turned her face to the wall and wouldn't say another word.

What was the Tsar to do? He called together his councilors and asked them how was the Princess to be made to laugh. The councilors were wise about state matters but not one of them could suggest a means of amusing the Princess. The Master of Ceremonies did indeed begin to say something about a nice young man but instantly the Tsar roared out such a wrathful, "Wow! Wow!" that the Master of Ceremonies coughed and pretended he hadn't spoken.

Then the Tsar called together the scholars and the teachers and the first lady-in-waiting. He glared at them savagely and roared, "Wow! Wow! A nice lot you are! I put you in charge of my daughter and not one of you has sense enough to know that the poor child needs a little amusement! I have a good mind to have you all thrown into the dungeon!"

"But, Your Majesty," quavered one poor old scholar, "I was not employed as a buffoon but as a teacher of astrology!"

"And I," another said, "as a teacher of languages!"

"And I as a teacher of philosophy!"

"Silence!" roared the Tsar. "Between you all you have about killed my poor child! Now I ask you: With all your learning doesn't one of you know how to make a young girl laugh?"

Apparently not one of them did, for no one answered.

"Not even you?" the Tsar said, looking at the first lady-in-waiting.

"When you called me to Court," the first lady-in-waiting answered, drawing herself up in a most refined manner, "you said you wished me to teach your daughter etiquette. As you said nothing about amusement, quite naturally I confined myself to the subject of behavior. If I do say it myself, no one has ever been more devoted to duty than I. I am constantly saying to her: 'That isn't the way a princess should act!' In fact for years there has hardly been a moment in the day when I haven't corrected her for something!"

"Poor child!" groaned the Tsar. "No wonder she wants a change! Oh, what fools you all are in spite of your learning! Don't you know that a young girl is a young girl even if she is a princess!"

Well, the scholars weren't any more help to the Tsar than the councilors, and finally in desperation he sent heralds through the land to announce that to any one who could make the Princess laugh he would give three bags of gold.

Three bags of gold don't grow on the bushes every day and instantly all the youths and men and old men who had stories that their sweethearts and their wives and their daughters laughed at hurried to the castle.

One by one they were admitted to the Princess's chamber. They entered hopefully but when they saw the Tsar sitting at one side of the door muttering. "Wow! Wow!" in his beard, and the old first lady-in-waiting at the other side of the door watching them scornfully, and the Princess herself in bed with her lovely hair spread out like a golden fan on the pillow, they forgot their funny stories and hemmed and hawed and stammered and had finally, one after another, to be turned out in disgrace.

One day went by and two and three and still the Princess refused to eat. In despair the Tsar sent out his heralds again. This time he said that to any one who would make the Princess laugh he would give the Princess's hand in marriage and make him joint heir to the kingdom.

"I had expected to wed her to the son of some great Tsar," he sighed, "but I'd rather marry her to a farmer than see her die of starvation!"

The heralds rode far and wide until every one,

even the people on the most distant farms, had heard of the Tsar's offer.

"I won't try again," said Mihailo, the oldest son of the farmer I've already told you about. "When I went there the day before yesterday I began telling her a funny story out of my Latin book but instead of laughing she said, 'Oh, send him away!' So now she'll have to starve to death for all of me!"

"Me, too!" said Jakov, the second son. "When I tried to tell her that funny story of how I traded the moldy oats for the old widow's fat pig, instead of laughing she looked me straight in the face and said, 'Cheat!'"

"Stefan ought to go," Mihailo suggested. "Maybe she'd laugh at him! Everybody else does!"

He spoke sneeringly but Stefan only smiled.

"Who knows? Perhaps I will go. If I do make her laugh then, O my brothers, the laugh will be on you for I shall become Tsar and you two will be known as my two poor brothers. Ho! Ho! Ho! What a joke that would be!"

Stefan laughed loud and heartily and his little sister joined him, but his brothers looked at him sourly.

"He grows more foolish all the time!" they told each other.

When they were gone to bed, Militza slipped over to Stefan and whispered in his ear, "Brother, you must go to the Princess. Tell her the story that begins: In my young days when I was an old, old man. . . . I think she'll just have to laugh, and if she laughs then she can eat and she must be very hungry by this time."

At first Stefan said no, he wouldn't go, but Militza insisted and finally, to please her, he said he would.

So early the next morning he dressed himself in his fine Sunday shirt with its blue and red embroidery. He put on his bright red Sunday sash and his long shiny boots. Then he mounted his horse and before his brothers were awake rode off to the Tsar's castle.

There he awaited his turn to be admitted to the Princess's chamber. When he came in he was so young and healthy and vigorous that he seemed to bring with him a little of the freshness of outdoors. The first lady-in-waiting looked at him askance for without doubt he was a farmer lad and his table manners probably were not good. Well, he was a farmer lad and for that reason he didn't know that she was first lady-in-waiting. He glanced at her once and thought, "What an ugly old woman!" and thereafter he didn't think of her at all. He glanced likewise at the Tsar and the Tsar reminded him of a bull of his own. He wasn't afraid of the bull, so why be afraid of the Tsar?

Suddenly he saw the Princess lying in bed with her lovely hair spread out on the pillow like a golden fan and for a moment he couldn't speak. Then he knelt beside the bed and kissed her hand.

"Princess," he said, "I'm not learned and I'm not clever and I don't suppose I can succeed where so many wise men have failed. And even if I do make you laugh you won't have to marry me unless you want to because the reason I really came was to please Militza."

"Militza?"

"Yes, Princess, my little sister, Militza. She loves me very much and so she thinks the stories I tell are funny and she laughs at them. Last night she said to me, 'Stefan, you must go to the Princess and tell her the story that begins: In my young days when I was an old, old man . . . I think she'll just have to laugh and if she laughs then she can eat and she must be very hungry by this time.'"

"I am," the Princess said, with a catch in her voice. Then she added, "I think I like that little sister of yours and I think I like you, too. I wish you would tell me the story that begins: In my young days when I was an old, old man. . . ."

"But, Princess, it's a very foolish story."

"The foolisher, the better!"

Just here the first lady-in-waiting tried to correct the Princess for of course she should have said, "The more foolish, the better!" but the Tsar shut her up with a black frown and one fierce, "Wow!"

Stefan began:

In my young days when I was an old, old man I used to count my bees every morning. It was easy enough to count the bees but not the beehives because I had too many hives. One day when I finished counting I found that my best bee was missing. At once I saddled a rooster and set out to find him.

"Father!" cried the Princess, "did you hear what Stefan said? He said he saddled his rooster!"

"Umph!" muttered the Tsar, and the first lady-in-waiting said severely, "Princess, do not interrupt! Young man, continue."

His track led to the sea which I rode across on a bridge. The first thing I saw on the other side of the sea was my bee. There he was in a field of millet harnessed to a plow. "That's my bee!" I shouted to the man who was driving him. "Is that so?" the man said, and without any words he gave me back my bee and handed me a bag of millet to pay for the plowing. I took the bag and tied it securely on the bee. The rooster, poor thing, was so tired that I had to take him by the hand and lead him along beside us.

"Father!" the Princess cried, "did you hear that? He took the rooster by the hand! Isn't that funny?"

"Umph!" grunted the Tsar, and the first lady-in-waiting whispered, "Hush! Let the young man finish!"

Whilst we were crossing the bridge, the string of the bag broke and all my millet spilled out. When night came I tied the rooster to the bee and lay down on the seashore to sleep. During the night some wolves came and killed my bee and when I woke up I found that all the honey had run out of his body. There was so much honey that it rose up and up until it reached the ankles of the valleys and the knees of the mountains. I took a hatchet and swam down to a forest where I found two deer leaping about on one leg. I shot at the deer with my hatchet, killed them, and skinned them. With the skins I made two leather bottles. I filled these with the honey and strapped them over the rooster's back. Then I rode home. I no sooner arrived home than my father was born. "We must have holy water for the christening," I said. "I suppose I must go to heaven to fetch some." But how was I to get there? I thought of my millet. Sure enough, the dampness had made it grow so well that its tops now reached the sky. So all I had to do was to climb a millet stalk and there I was in heaven. Up there they had mown down some of my millet which they baked into a loaf and were eating with boiled milk. "That's my millet!" I said. "What do you want for it?" they asked me. "I want some holy water to christen my father who has just been born." So they gave me some holy water and I prepared to descend again to earth. But on earth there was a violent storm going on and the wind carried away my millet. So there I was with no way of getting down. I thought of my hair. It was so long that when I stood up it covered my ears and when I lay down it reached all the way to earth. So I pulled out a hair, tied it to a tree of heaven, and began descending by it. When it grew dark I made a knot in the hair and just sat where I was. It was cold, so I took a needle which I happened to have in my coat, split it up, and lighted a fire with the chips.

"Oh, father!" the Princess cried, "Stefan says he split a needle into kindling wood! Isn't he funny!"

"If you ask me—" the first lady-in-waiting began, but before she could say more the Tsar reached over and stepped on her toe so hard that she was forced to end her sentence with a little squeally, "Ouch!" The Princess, you see, was smiling and the Tsar was hoping that presently she would burst into a laugh. So he motioned Stefan to continue.

Then I lay down beside the fire and fell asleep. While I slept a spark from the fire fell on the hair and burned it through. I fell to earth with such force that

I sank into the ground up to my chest. I couldn't budge, so I was forced to go home and get a spade and dig myself out. On the way home I crossed a field where the reapers were cutting corn. The heat was so great that they had to stop work. "I'll get our mare," I said, "and then you'll feel cooler." You know our mare is two days' long and as broad as midnight and she has willow trees growing on her back. So I ran and got her and she cast such a cool shadow that the reapers were at once able to go back to work. Now they wanted some fresh drinking water, but when they went to the river they found it had frozen over. They came back to me and asked me would I get them some water. "Certainly," I said. I went to the river myself, then I took off my head and with it I broke a hole in the ice. After that it was easy enough to fetch them some water. "But where is your head?" they asked. "Oh," I said, "I must have forgotten it!"

"Oh, father!" the Princess cried with a loud laugh, "he says he forgot his head! Then, Stefan, what did you do? What did you do?"

I ran back to the river and got there just as a fox was sniffing at my skull. "Hi, there!" I said, pulling the fox's tail. The fox turned around and gave me a paper on which was written these words: NOW THE PRINCESS

CAN EAT FOR SHE HAS LAUGHED AND STEFAN AND HIS
LITTLE SISTER ARE VERY HAPPY.

"What nonsense!" the first lady-in-waiting murmured with a toss of her head.

"Yes, beautiful nonsense!" the Princess cried, clap-
ping her hands and going off into peal after peal of
merry laughter. "Isn't it beautiful nonsense, father?
And isn't Stefan a dear lad? And, father, I'm awfully
hungry! Please have some food sent in at once and
Stefan must stay and eat with me."

So the Tsar had great trays of food brought in:
roast birds and vegetables and wheaten bread and
many kinds of little cakes and honey and milk and
fruit. And Stefan and the Princess ate and made
merry and the Tsar joined them and even the first
lady-in-waiting took one little cake which she crum-
bled in her handkerchief in a most refined manner.

Then Stefan rose to go and the Tsar said to him,
"Stefan, I will reward you richly. You have made the
Princess laugh and besides you have not insisted on
her marrying you. You are a fine lad and I shall never
forget you."

"But, father," the Princess said, "I don't want
Stefan to go. He amuses me and I like him. He said
I needn't marry him unless I wanted to but, father,
I think I want to."

"Wow! Wow!" the Tsar roared. "What! My daughter marry the son of a farmer!"

"Now, father," the Princess said, "it's no use your *wow-wowing* at me and you know it isn't. If I can't marry Stefan I won't marry any one. And if I don't marry any one I'm going to stop eating again. So that's that!" And still holding Stefan's hand, the Princess turned her face to the wall.

What could the poor Tsar do? At first, he fumed and raged but as usual after a day or two he came around to the Princess's way of thinking. In fact it soon seemed to him that Stefan had been his choice from the first and when one of his councilors remarked, "Then, Your Majesty, there's no use sending word to the neighboring kings that the Princess has reached a marriageable age and would like to look over their sons," the Tsar flew into an awful temper and roared:

"Wow! Wow! You blockhead! Neighboring kings, indeed, and their good-for-nothing sons! No, siree! The husband I want for my daughter is an honest farmer lad who knows how to work and how to play! That's the kind of son-in-law we need in this kingdom!"

So Stefan and the little Princess were married and from that day the castle was no longer gloomy but rang with laughter and merriment. Presently the people of the kingdom, following the example of their rulers, were laughing, too, and cracking jokes and, strange to say, they soon found they were working all the better for their jollity.

Laughter grew so fashionable that even Mihailo and Jakov were forced to take it up. They didn't do it very well but they practiced at it conscientiously. Whenever people talked about Stefan, they always pushed forward importantly and said, "Ho! Ho! Ho! Do you mean Stefan, the Laughing Prince? Ha! Ha! Ha! Why, do you know, he's our own brother!"

As for Militza, the Princess had her come to the castle and said to her, "I owe all my happiness to you, my dear, for you it was who knew that of course I would laugh at Stefan's nonsense! What sensible girl wouldn't?"

The Emperor's New Clothes

Many years ago there lived an Emperor, who thought so much of grand new clothes that he spent all his money upon them, that he might be very fine. He did not care about his soldiers; he did not care to see the play or to drive in the woods, except to show his new clothes. He had a coat for every hour of the day; and just as they say of a king, "He is in council," so

they always said of him, "The Emperor is in the
clothes-closet."

In the great city in which he lived it was always
very merry. Every day came many strangers. One day
two rogues came: they gave themselves out as weavers, and said they knew how to weave the finest stuff
any one could fancy. Not only were their colors and
patterns, they said, very beautiful, but the clothes
made of the stuff had the wonderful quality that they
could not be seen by any one who was unfit for the
office he held, or was too stupid for anything.

"Those would be capital clothes!" thought the
Emperor. "If I wore those, I should be able to find
out what men in my empire were not fit for the places
they have; I could tell the clever from the dunces.
Yes, the stuff must be woven for me at once!" And he
gave the two rogues a great deal of cash in hand, that
they might begin their work without delay.

As for them, they put up two looms, and made as
if they were working; but they had nothing at all on
their looms. They at once called for the finest silk
and the costliest gold; this they put into their own
pockets, and worked at the empty looms till late into
the night.

"I should like to know how far they have got on
with the stuff," thought the Emperor. But he felt
quite uneasy when he thought that one who was

stupid or not fit for his office could not see it. He believed, indeed, that he had nothing to fear for himself; still he thought he had better first send some one else to see how matters stood. All the people in the city knew what peculiar power the stuff had, and all were anxious to see how bad or how stupid their neighbors were.

"I will send my honest old Minister to the weavers," thought the Emperor. "He can judge best how the stuff looks, for he has sense, and no one knows his place better than he."

Now the good old Minister went out into the hall where the two rogues sat working at the empty looms.

"Mercy on us!" thought the old Minister, and he opened his eyes wide. "I cannot see anything at all!" But he did not say this.

Both the rogues begged him to be so good as to come nearer, and asked if the colors and the patterns were not pretty. Then they pointed to the empty loom, and the poor old Minister went on opening his eyes; but he could see nothing, for there was nothing.

"Mercy!" thought he. "Suppose I am really stupid! I never thought that, and not a soul must know it. Suppose I am not fit for my office! No, it will never do for me to tell that I could not see the stuff."

"You don't say anything of it?" said one, as he went on weaving.

"Oh, it is charming,—quite enchanting!" said the old Minister, as he peered through his glasses. "What a fine pattern, and what colors! Yes, I shall tell the Emperor that I am very much pleased with it."

"Well, we are glad of that," said both the weavers; and then they named the colors, and explained the strange pattern. The old Minister listened closely, that he might be able to repeat it when he came to the Emperor. And he did so.

Now the rogues asked for more money, and silk and gold; they wanted it all for weaving. They put all into their own pockets, and not a thread was put upon the loom; but they kept by it as before, and wove at the empty loom.

The Emperor soon sent another honest officer of the court, to see how the weaving was going on, and if the stuff would soon be ready. He fared just like the first: he looked and looked, but, as there was nothing to be seen but the empty looms, he could see nothing.

"Is not that a pretty piece of stuff?" asked the two rogues; and they showed and made clear the handsome pattern which was not there at all.

"I am not stupid!" thought the man: "it must be my good office, for which I am not fit. That would be queer enough, but I must not let it be noticed." And so he praised the stuff which he did not see, and said how pleased he was with the beautiful colors and charming pattern. "Yes, it is enchanting," he told the Emperor.

All the people in the town talked of the gorgeous stuff.

Now, the Emperor wished to see it himself while it was still upon the loom. With a whole crowd of chosen men, among whom were also the two honest statesmen who had already been there, he went to the two cunning rogues, who were weaving with might and main without fibre or thread.

"Is not that splendid?" said the two honest statesmen. "Does Your Majesty see what a pattern it has and what colors?" And then they pointed to the empty loom, for they thought that the others could see the stuff.

"What's this?" thought the Emperor. "I can see nothing at all! That is terrible. Am I stupid? Am I not fit to be Emperor? That would be the most dreadful thing that could happen to me." "Oh, it is very pretty!" he said aloud. "It has my highest approval." And he nodded in a contented way, and gazed at the empty loom, for he would not say that he saw nothing. The whole crowd whom he had with him looked and looked, but they got nothing more out of it than all the rest; but, like the Emperor, they said, "Oh, that is very pretty!" And they begged him to have some clothes made of this new, pretty stuff, and to wear them for the first time in the great procession that was to take place. "It is splendid, excellent!" went from mouth to mouth, and they all were like one person in the way they talked. The Emperor gave each of the rogues a ribbon to wear in his buttonhole, and gave them the title of Imperial Court Weavers.

The whole night before the morning on which the procession was to take place, the rogues were up, and kept more than sixteen candles burning. The people could see that they were hard at work upon the Emperor's new clothes. They made believe to take the stuff down from the loom; they made cuts in the air with great shears; they sewed with needles without thread; and at last they said, "Now the clothes are ready!"

The Emperor came himself with his noblest cavaliers; and the two rogues lifted up one arm as if they were holding something, and said, "See, here are the trousers! here is the coat! here is the cape!" and so on. "It is as light as a spider's web: one would think one had nothing on; but that is just the beauty of it."

"Yes," said all the cavaliers; but they could not see anything, for there was nothing.

"Will Your Imperial Majesty be so good as to take

off your clothes?" said the rogues; "then we will put on you the new clothes here in front of the great mirror."

The Emperor took off his clothes, and the rogues pretended to put on him each new robe as it was ready; they wrapped him about and they tied and they buttoned, and they worked hard, and the Emperor turned round and round before the mirror.

"Oh, how well they look! how nicely they fit!" said all. "What a pattern! what colors! That *is* a splendid dress!"

"They are standing outside with the canopy which is to be borne above Your Majesty in the procession!" said the Head Master of the Ceremonies.

"Well, I am ready," replied the Emperor. "Does it not suit me well?" And then he turned again to the mirror, for he wanted it to look as if he saw all his finery.

The chamberlains, who were to carry the train, stooped down with their hands toward the floor, just as if they were picking up the train; then they held it up in the air. They did not dare to let it be seen that they could see nothing.

So the Emperor went in procession under the rich canopy, and all the people in the streets and at the windows said, "How fine the Emperor's new clothes are! what a train he has to his mantle! how well it fits him!" No one would let it be seen that he could see nothing, for that would have shown that he was not fit for his office, or was very stupid. No clothes of the Emperor's had ever had such a success as these.

"But he has nothing on!" said a little child.

"Mercy on us! Just hear that innocent voice!" said his father; and one whispered to another what the child had said.

"He has nothing on; there's a little child here says he has nothing on."

"That's so! he has nothing on!" said the people at last. That touched the Emperor, for it seemed to him that they were right; but he thought within himself, "I must go through with the procession." And so he held himself a little higher, and the chamberlains marched and carried the train, but there was no train.

Ah Mee's Invention

"A shamelessly rainy day, my honorable Brother Chi."

"That is truth, esteemed Brother Cha. It rains perfectly hard. There will be plenty of leisure in which to beat the children."

Ching Chi was merely quoting an old Swa Tou saying. Every one knows that on rainy days old and young are crowded, arm against elbow, in the house; often to get in each the other's way—and misunderstandings are likely to arise. Then the bamboo

116]

is brought into play—and there are wailings. That is how the Swa Tou saying originated. When Ching Chi used it, he did so in fun, and, no doubt, to make talk.

But Ching Cha thought his brother was speaking with earnestness. His face, made glum by the rain and by secret troubles, brightened at such a pleasing prospect. "Ho. Leisure to beat the children? What an utterly excellent idea. I, myself, will cut bamboos for your hand. Ah Mee is the one to beat. He played at being a mad wild elephant—oh, so perfectly wild, and with such trampling—in the midst of my *huang ya tsai* patch."

Ching Chi seemed altogether astonished. His face showed that he thought Ching Cha must be over-stepping the truth. "What? What do you say to me, honorable Brother Cha? Ah Mee playing wild elephant in your cabbage patch? But I thought that I told him, emphatically, to break no more of your cabbages."

"It is no blemish upon my lips. It is the truth," said Ching Cha sullen and hurt because Chi disbelieved. "He played elephant in my cabbages. Come and I will show you."

"Oh, no." Ching Chi shook his head. "It is raining far too hard. I'll speak of the matter again to my son."

Ching Cha adjusted his *wei li* (rain hat) the

straighter and shuffled off through the downpour. As he went he muttered something that sounded like "*Wou tou meng.*" If that is what he really said, he called Ching Chi a stupid old noddy.

But Ching Chi merely laughed. He had no intention of beating Ah Mee, his "pearl in the palm," his son.

Now whether Ching Chi was right or wrong is a pretty question. Some persons answer it one way, and some, another. But there was no question about this. . . . Ah Mee was terrible. If anything, he was as bad as that lazy Ah Fun, son of Dr. Chu Ping. Here is their only difference. Ah Fun never did what he was told to do. Ah Mee always did what he was told *not* to do. But he did it in such a manner as to leave a loophole. He always had a perfectly good excuse. Take the matter of his uncle Ching Cha's cabbage patch. . . .

Only a day or so before, Ah Mee had pretended that he was a fierce and furious dragon—a *loong.* As a fierce and furious dragon, he threshed this way and that through Uncle Ching Cha's very delectable cabbages—causing much hurt. Ching Chi, the parent, told Ah Mee never again to play dragon in Uncle Cha's cabbages. "Ah Mee, you must never again play dragon in your honorable uncle's cabbage patch. If **you** do, I shall speak to you most sharply." And Ah

Mee said, "Yes, sir," and obeyed. He pretended to be a ferocious wild elephant. He didn't play dragon again. *Oh, no. Not at all. He was very careful not even to think of a dragon.* He was a weighty elephant —amid the cabbages.

Ching Chi, the fond parent, lived with his wife— her name is forgotten—and the son, Ah Mee, and a little daughter, in a neat house that stood in the Street of The Hill Where The Monkey Bit Mang. Ching Chi was a carver of wood, and ivory, and jade. His bachelor brother Ching Cha who lived next door, did scrivening—wrote things with a blackened brush upon parchment and paper—and the wall, when he had no paper. Some people said they were stories, but certainly they brought in no money. As for that, neither did Ching Chi's carvings bring in any money. Yet Chi was a good carver. His designs were artistic, and his knife was obedient to the slightest touch. From an inch block of ivory he could carve seven balls—one inside the other. Howbeit, Chi was neither famous nor wealthy. Instead of carving pagodas and trinkets for sale in the bazaars, he spent most of his time in carving toys for Ah Mee—who promptly smote them with an axe, or threw them in the well, or treated them in some other manner equally grievous.

For six months Ching Chi worked to carve a dragon. When finished, the *loong* was a thing of beauty. In the bazaar it would, perhaps, have fetched a bar of silver from some rich mandarin. But fond Ching Chi gave it to Ah Mee. And Ah Mee, tiring of it after five minutes of play, hurled it through the paper-covered window.

Are windows made to be broken? Are toys fashioned only to be thrown away? Certainly not. Papa Chi wagged a finger at Ah Mee and he spoke thus, "Ah Mee, most wonderful son in the world, you must not throw your dragon through the window into the back yard again. What I say, that I mean. Don't throw your dragon into the yard any more." Having said, he proceeded with his work, carving beautiful designs upon teakwood blocks . . . for Ah Mee's pleasure.

And Ah Mee said, "Very well then, *Tieh tieh* (Daddy), I won't." He proceeded with his work—which was to pile carven teakwood blocks high as his not-so-long arms could reach. There was one block covered with so much exquisite carving that it gave little support to the blocks above. For that reason the tower wavered and fell. Ah Mee promptly lost his temper. Made furious beyond endurance, he seized the offending block and hurled it through a paper-paneled door.

Who will say that Ah Mee was disobedient? He had been told not to throw his toy dragon through

the window. But had his father, Ching Chi, told him
not to heave a *block* through the *door*? Not at all.
Ching Chi had said nothing about blocks, and he had
pointed his finger at the window. Nevertheless, Mr.
Ching felt almost inclined to scold his son. He said,
very sternly, "Ah Mee. . . ."

"Whang! Bang! Bang!" came the sound of sticks on
the door frame. Crash—the door flew open. In rushed
stalwart men, dressed in the King's livery, and bearing heavy staves. "Oh, you vile *tung hsi* (east west—
very abusive talk), you murderer," screamed the
men. "Are you trying to assassinate your King? What
do you mean by hurling missiles into the King's sedan
as he is carried through the streets? Answer, before
your head falls."

But Ching Chi was unable to answer. He could only
press his forehead to the floor, and tremble, and wait
for the quick death he expected. Meantime, Ah Mee
pelted the King's men with various large and small
toys—including a hatchet.

King Tan Ki, seated comfortably in a sedan chair,
was being carried through the Street Of The Hill
Where The Monkey Bit Mang. He had no thought of
danger. Peril had no place in his mind. The street
seemed a street of peace. When lo—from a paper-
covered door there came a large missile, striking a
slave and falling into the King's lap. Instantly the

bodyguard rushed to the terrible house and battered in the door. But King Tan Ki felt more curiosity than alarm. He examined the object that had so unceremoniously been hurled into the sedan. At once his interest was quickened. The King knew good carvings—whether they came from old masters, or from hands unknown. Here was a block carved with superlative art. Tan Ki wished to know more of the artist who carved it.

Ching Chi was still kneeling, still expecting instant death, when the King's chamberlain rushed in. The chamberlain uttered a sharp order. The bodyguards grasped Ching Chi and hastened him out of the house, to kneel at the King's sedan. Ah Mee fired a last volley of broken toys at the retreating chamberlain. . . . Not especially nice of him, perhaps, but then, no one had forbidden it.

Fortune had smiled her prettiest upon the house of Ching Chi. King Tan Ki was immensely pleased with the old engraver's work. The odds and ends of toys that had been fashioned for Ah Mee, now graced the palace. There they were appreciated. Every day Ching Chi worked faithfully, carving plaques and panels and medallions for the King. He was wealthy. Upon his little skullcap was a red button. He was a mandarin, if you please. Only mandarins of the highest class may wear ruby buttons on their caps. . . .

And Ah Mee was worse than ever.

To say it again, for emphasis, Ah Mee was worse than ever—if possible. He dabbled in all the hundred-and-one varieties of mischief. All day long it was "Ah Mee, don't do that." "Ah Mee, don't do the other." "Don't. Don't. Don't." Papa Ching was so tired of saying "Don't" that his tongue hurt every time he said the word. Occasionally he changed his talk and said the opposite of what he really meant. Thus he would say, "That's right, little darling, fill papa's boots with hop toads and muddy terrapins, and that will make papa happy." Or, "Pray, take another jar, my precious. Eat all the jam you possibly can. Six jars is not at all too much." For Ah Mee doted on jam. It was a passion with him. He started the day on jam, finished the day on jam. Every time a back was turned, his fingers sought the jam pot. Indeed, rather frequently he ate so much jam that there were pains . . . and the doctor.

Ching Chi took a bird cage from the wall and hung it on his arm. (In that land when gentlemen go for a stroll they usually carry their pet larks, instead of their pet *chous*.) At the door he turned and said to Ah Mee: "Little pearl in the palm, please refrain from too much mischief. Don't (there it was again) be any worse than you are really compelled to be Of course, it's quite proper for you to put arsenic in

Mother's tea, and to hit baby sister with the axe again.
And you may burn the house if you feel so inclined.
. . . I want you to have plenty of innocent fun. But
don't (again) be bad. For instance, don't, I beg of
you, don't get in those jars of jam any more."

Off went Ching Chi with his lark singing blithely.

Ah Mee was quite puzzled. "Don't get in the jars
of jam." How in the world *could* he get in the little
jars? It was silly. He was much larger than any one
of the jars. But perhaps *Tieh tieh* meant not put a
hand in the jars. That must be it. Ah Mee made a
stern resolve to keep his hands out. Not so much as
a finger should go in those jars. . . .

Obedient Ah Mee arranged several of his father's
carven plaques on the floor, and tilted a jar. The
plaques were beautifully decorated flat pieces of
wood, somewhat larger than dinner plates. They
made reasonably good dishes for the stiff jam. Sur-
rounded by little mountains of jam, Ah Mee sat on
the floor and . . . how the mountains disappeared.
Really, it was fairish tasting jam.

When Ching Chi came home and discovered his
carvings smeared with black and sticky jam, that good
soul fell into a passion. First he screamed. Next he
howled. *Then he seized the plaques and flung them
from him,* flung them with all his strength. Flinging
seems to have been a family failing.

Ching Chi was weeping for sorrow, and howling with rage when his brother Cha entered the room. The quick eyes of Brother Cha soon saw that some-thing was amiss. He gazed at the jam-coated plaques. Then he too howled, but with joy. "Oh, Brother Chi," he shouted, "you have chanced upon a won-derful invention. What huge luck." He led Brother Chi to the wall and pointed. "See. For reason of its jam, each plaque has made a black impression on the wall. Every line of the carving is reproduced upon the wall. Now do you understand? You will carve my thoroughly miserable stories upon blocks of wood. Ah Mee will spread black jam upon the carven blocks. Then I will press the blocks upon paper, sheet after sheet, perhaps a hundred in one day. . . . With the laborious brush I can make only one story a month. With the blocks—I can make thousands. Oh, what a wonderful invention!"

Ching Chi carved his brother's stories upon wooden blocks. Ah Mee spread the jam thickly—only pausing now and then for a taste. Ching Cha pressed the blocks upon paper, sheet after sheet. . . . There were the stories upon paper—all done in a twinkling, and with little expense. The poorest people in the land could afford to buy Ching Cha's most excellent stories.

Thus was invented *Yin Shu* (Make Books) or, as

the very odd foreign demons call it in their so peculiar language—"Printing." Ching Chi, his brother Ching Cha, and Ah Mee, all had a hand in the invention. As a matter of exact truth, Ah Mee had two hands in the invention (or in the jam), so he is generally given all the credit. His monument reads, "Ah Mee, the Inventor of Printing."

The Ghost's Ghost

A mile above the Drake Hotel on Tobago, the island rises from coral sand to thickly forested hills. As the beach disappears from the water-edge, high stone cliffs take its place. The first of these cliffs reaches out into the sea and the blue-green water below beats on it. This is called Pirate's Point, once a favorite gathering place for the boys of the island. Here they would sit by day and throw stones down into the water and pretend to be killing sharks. None of them would go there at night; an old island legend said that at night the Point is haunted.

The Point was closed off to everyone a little while

ago when a Mr. Crumpf from America bought it and built a house just forty feet from the edge. His house was one story high, with a veranda that overlooked the edge of the cliff and the sea. Over the house was the shade of palms and the deep green shadows of breadfruit trees. The people on the island watched the building of the house but they said to each other that in spite of the house and in spite of Mr. Crumpf, the Point would remain haunted.

Mouseknees sat at the Point one afternoon, uncon-cerned about Mr. Crumpf's roadway sign: Private Property. He and Mr. Crumpf were friends. On this afternoon Mouseknees was just lying in the sun too lazy to sit up and look down at the water below. His goat, Pahdetoo, was beside him, even more content to lie in the sun. He had looked over the edge of the cliff and had tried to get a stalk of grass growing a foot below the edge. Mouseknees had yanked him back by the rope collar around his neck and Pahdetoo lost all interest in the edge and what might be over it. But the collar had broken and Mouseknees now re-peated idly, "Wish I had a goat collar! A shiny leather goat collar!" Pahdetoo said nothing.

Fifty feet away old Crawfoot, who could be per-suaded to do odd jobs only when he felt like it, was mowing a very poor lawn. It was a new lawn, just planted when Mr. Crumpf finished the house two months ago. Every four feet Crawfoot stopped, scratched his head, wiped his forehead, blinked three or four times, took several deep breaths, and then leaned against the handle of the mower. After a dozen pauses, he called, "What you doin', Mouseknees?"

"Nothin'."

That satisfied Crawfoot for twelve more feet and three pauses. Then he asked, "You got nothin' to do?"

"Nothin'."

Crawfoot pushed the mower ahead, then stopped as if he had just thought of something. "You can't sit there much longer. You can't sit there next week."

"Wasn't goin' to sit that long. Must be at the hotel at five."

"You can't even come here next week."

"Why not?" Mouseknees asked lazily.

"People comin' here to live. Mr. Crumpf let the house. Mighty rich people comin' here from England to live."

Mouseknees sat up. That was news and he was surprised that he had not heard it before. News gets around Tobago about as fast as it takes the wind to blow it. He thought about the news for a little while, then he asked, "Who's the people?"

Crawfoot put down the mower and walked over with the air of a man bearing an important secret. "Anna tole me." Anna was Mr. Crumpf's cook. "She say Mr. and Mrs. Kidley-Plinker comin' to spend de winter."

"Who's that, Kidley-Plinker?"

"That's the name of the people comin'."

"Sounds like names enough for two people."

"If they want three names they don't ask you," Crawfoot said. "They come on the boat this week an' stay the winter in the house here."

"Where Mr. Crumpf go?"

"He stay in de hotel. But Marie who is cook for Mr. Smith tell me she hear from John who runs a taxi that he hear someone say that they hear that Mr. Crumpf awful sorry now he let he house."

"Lots of people do lots of talkin'," Mouseknees laughed.

"Man no talk, news can't go," Crawfoot said.

"Crawfoot!" That was a roar from the house. "I thought I told you to get that grass cut in a hurry."

Mouseknees turned around and smiled at Mr. Crumpf. He was a little man with a broad head, a round red face that was redder than usual, and a short thick neck.

"Hello, Mouseknees," Mr. Crumpf said. "Want some candy?" He held out a bag. "You better run along and not hinder Crawfoot at his work. He hinders awful easy!"

When Mouseknees came to the hotel each morning before seven, Pahdetoo followed behind, usually annoyed at being snatched from one clump of roadside grass after another. Mouseknees had made him a new rope collar. Since the goat was forbidden on the hotel grounds Mouseknees tied him to a hedge at the end of the field behind the hotel where no one could see him. No one knew that the goat was here. Here he could graze all day.

On the morning when the weekly steamer was due Mouseknees came to the hotel especially early. New guests would arrive and there was pleasant confusion, and new guests were always fun. He hurried to the hedge and tied the goat, then went to work.

The veranda had to be scrubbed, the tables in the dining room had to be set for breakfast. Water glasses had to be filled and napkins had to be folded. Just as the work was done the ship whistled at the harbor.

A half hour later automobiles came to the back of the hotel and Mouseknees heard new and strange voices. Looking down from the veranda he saw several new couples but the couple with Mr. Crumpf interested him most. They were a large, tall woman and a stout man who puffed when he talked. Beside them was Mr. Crumpf, looking rather proud and acting very busy.

Mrs. Hudson called to all the boys, "Hurry down

and help with the baggage." Mouseknees went to the automobiles. A large pile of bags was waiting and boys were loading themselves from it. Mouseknees picked up two bags at random, one large, one very small.

"Look here, boy," Mr. Kidley-Plinker said. "Be careful with that small bag and look sharp."

"Yes, sir," Mouseknees smiled.

Pigeon started upstairs, his arms filled with bags. As he passed Mouseknees he said, "Picked the littlest?"

"I did not!" Mouseknees wanted to race after Pigeon. Then, before he could stop it, the smallest bag slid from his hand, hit the stairs, and opened. A dozen jars and bottles rattled down the steps and crashed against the pavement.

"My wife's toilet articles," Mr. Kidley-Plinker shouted. In the confusion, everybody began running after rolling jars, running for brooms, while a dozen people started to talk at once. And Mouseknees wished that he were far, far away.

Mrs. Kidley-Plinker's voice was the loudest. "The idea! Outrageous!" She stalked over to Mouseknees. "You—you careless boy!"

"I'm so sorry," Mrs. Hudson said, frowning at Mouseknees.

Mouseknees said nothing. He heard other boys

snickering at him and that hurt. Then he looked up and saw that Mr. Crumpf was smiling at him. He did not understand but he felt a little better, although he was sure that Mrs. Hudson would punish him.

"You clean up all this mess, Victor," Mrs. Hudson said. "Then you go weed the flower beds all morning!"

That would be punishment enough.

He began work at the flower beds by the edge of the porch. At least, he would not have to weed during the afternoon when the sun was really hot. The porch above him was filled with people and he could hear voices and it was sometimes amusing to listen to the chatter of the guests. The clearest voices now were those of Mr. Crumpf and Mrs. Kidley-Plinker. Mr. Crumpf was telling about his house.

"It's small, of course, but very comfortable," he said.

"I am sure it is," the lady answered.

"The point is beautiful. The place is called Pirate's Point."

"Indeed?" Mrs. Kidley-Plinker seemed interested. "And why should it be called that?"

"It's rather usual, isn't it," her husband interrupted, "that the place should have some name or other?"

"There's a legend about the place," Mr. Crumpf explained. "The natives of Tobago believe that the place is haunted."

Mouseknees could have corrected him. The place was haunted—he had been told so a hundred times.

"It seems that the crew of a pirate ship once threw their captain overboard as they were passing Tobago and then they came ashore to bury their treasure," Mr. Crumpf continued. "Ever since then the captain's ghost has been coming to the Point to hunt around and see if he can discover just where the treasure is buried."

"How ridiculous!" Mrs. Kidley-Plinker said. "And do the people really believe such nonsense?"

"There is much superstition on all the West Indian Islands."

Mouseknees, bent over a row of petunias, frowned. That story was not ridiculous and he knew it. Just because this lady came from England! He could name at least five people who knew people who knew people who had known people who had met the pirate captain on the Point. It would serve the lady right, for carrying little bags filled with bottles and jars, if the captain called on her.

The more he thought about that, the more amused

he was. Then he realized that he knew very little about the ghost of the captain. In fact, he knew very little about ghosts in general.

In the early afternoon, when he was free, he went directly to Mr. Crumpf's house. There would be no one around but Crawfoot, for Mr. Crumpf had taken the Colonel and his wife for a drive around the island. Crawfoot was still cutting grass. Mouseknees went to him, a question all ready.

"Crawfoot, what's a ghost?"

Crawfoot smiled as if he was glad for a chance to talk. "Well, a ghost is when you see something that ain't."

That was not very clear. "If it ain't, then how can you see it?"

"That's difficult," Crawfoot admitted. "A ghost would have to explain that to you. Only they know why that's so."

"Huh!" Mouseknees was puzzled. "Have you ever seen one?"

Crawfoot thought for a moment. "Well, yes an' no."

"How can you see a ghost yes and no?"

"I mean," Crawfoot explained, "that I seen things I thought was ghosts but I never stayed long enough to see if they was really ghosts."

"Why not?"

"It was too risky," Crawfoot admitted. "Supposin'

I was seein' somethin' what ain't, then there wouldn't be much danger. But supposin' I was seein' somethin' what is?"

Mouseknees nodded. "That would be bad."

"Worse'n bad! And that's why you can't ever take chances with a ghost. That's why it's always best to run fast."

"Did you ever see the captain here on the Point?"

Crawfoot shook his head. "Never did, but he's the worst kind of ghost. He's the kind you can't even see. You just hear him. My father knew a man whose brother was comin' along the road one night an' the captain talked to him."

"What did he say?"

"The man couldn't remember. He run so fast he shook the words right out of his ears."

"Humpf!" Mouseknees tried to picture the words falling to the road as the man ran on. "Mrs. Kidley-Plinker say she don't believe in ghosts."

"Such people," Crawfoot admitted, "say that only because they never met any. Anyway, she's a funny woman. Mr. Crumpf bring her here this mornin'. She look all around and she say the house is small, she got no room for all the servants she needs. An' she say she sorry this isn't here an' that isn't there an' this is too high an' that is too low an' this is too big an' that is too small an' this is wrong an' that is wrong an' those is wrong."

"What did Mr. Crumpf do?" Mouseknees felt sorry for him.

"He just nod an' nod, like Pahdetoo trying to scratch under his chin. An' he got redder an' redder an' redder but he just hold his tongue behin' his teeth. Anna say she bet he sorry he was so eager to rent he house without seein' these people first. She bet he break the lease if he could."

That did not concern Mouseknees and he only grunted. It certainly did not concern ghosts either and that was what interested him. "Tell me more about ghosts," he said. "Where do they live, what do they do, what do they wear, what do they eat?"

"I gotta get this grass cut," Crawfoot said. "Only a ghost can tell you those things."

The next morning, as he walked to the hotel with Pahdetoo, Mouseknees was still wondering about how you could see something that ain't. Crawfoot had only made the whole matter of ghosts more confusing.

"Oh, boy!" Behind him was Mrs. Kidley-Plinker, out taking an early morning walk. "Aren't you the one who dropped my bag yesterday?"

"Yes, ma'am!" He felt very uneasy.

"I understand you were punished for it. I am sure it was an accident."

"Yes, ma'am."

She asked him his name and his age and where he lived and what his father did. Mouseknees answered as briefly as possible. He was always timid when speaking to guests. He was very glad when they reached the hotel. As he went to the back hedge to tie Pahdetoo, he wished he had asked her about ghosts, but he was sure that he could not learn very much from her about them.

He tied Pahdetoo tight and was patting him for the last time when he heard a noise behind him. He turned and saw Pigeon.

"So this is where you keep your goat!"

Mouseknees did not answer.

"You better tie him tight so he don't get loose."

"He tied all right," Mouseknees said carelessly. Then, still eager for all information, he asked, "What's a ghost?"

"A ghost is something you wouldn't understand," Pigeon said loftily.

Mouseknees was not discouraged. "Have you ever seen the captain on Pirate's Point?"

"Seen him?" Pigeon laughed. "You know how close

a mango skin is to the seed? I was that close to him ten times."

"And you didn't run?"

"Why should I run?"

"Crawfoot say he always run."

Pigeon snorted. "Crawfoot got no more courage than a dead goat. A very dead goat."

"Crawfoot say a ghost is someone who ain't," Mouseknees said.

"He don't know nothin'. A ghost is someone who is but who looks as if he ain't."

That only made it more complicated.

"You wait, you see some day," Pigeon continued. "An' when you see a ghost, you run, too."

"Maybe, maybe not."

"You run so fast, you bump into the back of your head," Pigeon said. "You ever been on Pirate's Point at night?"

Mouseknees had to admit, "No, never."

"I bet you afraid to go there tonight."

"I got no reason to go," Mouseknees said carelessly.

"Victor!" Mrs. Hudson was calling from the veranda. "Come in and get to work!"

Certainly, this was no time to ask Mrs. Hudson about ghosts, either.

That morning Mouseknees helped take Mrs. Kidley-Plinker's baggage to the automobile. She was moving at once to Mr. Crumpf's house. Mouseknees heard her say, "The next time we sign no lease until we see the house."

"I told you that, my dear," her husband said. "Personally, I don't care for the whole island."

"What's wrong with it?"

"It's so small—there's water all around it."

"What do you expect on an island?"

"I mean, there's water everywhere you look. I fancy I shall get rather tired of it."

Mouseknees smiled at them as they drove away. Now Mr. Crumpf would come to live at the hotel and that was a good exchange.

When the last plate was put away in the china closet that night Mouseknees' work was done. He had hoped to see Mr. Crumpf at dinner but Mr. Crumpf was having a last dinner at his house with the new tenants.

Mouseknees left the hotel singing softly to himself, " 'Twas love an' love alone that cause' King Edward to leave the throne." It was one of the local songs. He came to the hedge where he had tied Pahdetoo but the goat was not visible in the darkness. Mouseknees reached down for the rope. Pahdetoo

had probably slipped under the hedge and Mouseknees called him softly. The rope was not there.

At first Mouseknees was terrified. Pahdetoo had
never gone off like this before. He might have been
stolen, he might have wandered away. In either case
he could not find him on a dark night for he could
not run over the island shouting, "Pahdetoo!" He
walked around the field but Pahdetoo was nowhere
around. He would have to wait until morning and
get up at dawn and search. Then Mouseknees knew
that if someone kept him tied in a field all day he
would be worse than lonely by nightfall. Perhaps
Pahdetoo had gone home out of simple impatience.
There was really no need to worry until he went home
and made sure that the goat was not there.

He came to the back of the hotel quietly. He did
not feel like singing now, for he was not certain that
Pahdetoo knew the road home.

Sitting on the back steps of the hotel was Pigeon.
"What's the matter, Mouseknees?"

"Nothing."

"Where's your goat?"

"He didn't feel well and he went home," Mouseknees said stoutly.

"Yeah!" That was half laugh, half snort.

Mouseknees was at once suspicious. "You know
where he is?"

"Sure," Pigeon said bluntly. "I was just waitin' to tell you but you wouldn't give me time. He's on Pirate's Point, in the shed back of Mr. Crumpf's house!"

Mouseknees felt his throat tighten. "Who put him there?"

"He didn't feel so well, just as you said, so I took him there after dinner," Pigeon laughed. "You go get him, Mouseknees, an' maybe you find out about ghosts. Maybe you meet the captain on the Point. It's a nice dark night an' he like dark nights. You make sure you say hello to him for me. Tell him Pigeon sends his best respects." And Pigeon walked off, whistling.

It was a dark night. It did Mouseknees no good to tell himself that since there were people in Mr. Crumpf's house, there was no need to worry about the dark and the ghost on the Point. The ghost was not afraid of people, else Crawfoot and Pigeon would never have met him. To get to that shed he would have to pass the darkest and the loneliest spot on the Point and he had never been on the Point at night. And if the thought of a meeting with that ghost were not bad enough, he had to chance meeting Mr. Crumpf who would be angry at him for coming there at night, or meeting the Kidley-Plinkers who would certainly report him to Mrs. Hudson! Then he decided he could go to Mr. Crumpf and ask for help and he felt better: but Pigeon would call him a coward and would always remind him of it. It would be best to go to the Point in the morning. Yet, if Pahdec too stayed there all night, without food and water—! Mouseknees thought of that once, twice, then started out for Pirate's Point.

Pigeon saw him go. "That ghost is particularly fond of small boys," he called.

"So long as he don't like small goats," Mouseknees answered.

He thought of the ghost all the way to the house, along the mile of main road to the gate, then along the drive in to the house. Trees took strange shapes, bushes became terrifying beings. But as he came near the house something more important pushed aside the thought of the ghost: he could hear voices from the veranda. To be caught now meant explanations and probably more trouble.

The side of the house toward the road was dark and he went along carefully. Fifty feet away, he saw the shed. This meant fifty feet of open lawn but he ran across it quickly and came to the shed door. He listened carefully to the voices on the veranda. He could hear their words and none of them indicated that he had been seen.

The shed was dark. A concrete-mixer occupied much of it, then a box filled with tools. In the darkness Mouseknees worked his way carefully to the rear and whispered, "Pahdetoo!" There was a silence, then a low soft, "Baah!" The goat was in a corner, tied to a workbench. Now, with Pahdetoo's rope in his hand, Mouseknees was afraid again. Here was darkness at Pirate's Point and in that darkness might be the ghost. He walked carefully to the doorway, the goat following behind.

Then Mouseknees jumped at least a foot. Behind him was a terrible clatter as Pahdetoo bumped into a worktable and upset a large tin pan. Mouseknees spun around and rushed to the rear of the shed. The ghost was forgotten: the worry now was Mr. Crumpf and Mouseknees could hear himself breathe.

Outside the shed, on the gravel walk, was the sound of footsteps. In the doorway of the shed, dim against the blue black sky, was Mr. Crumpf.

"Who's in here?" he asked angrily.

It would be better to answer than to stay silent and be discovered. "Me," Mouseknees said.

"Who's me?"

"Mouseknees!" It was best to confess. "My goat— the ghost on Pirate Point—Pigeon!" The whole confession came tumbling out and did not make much sense. Mouseknees was ready to begin again when

Mr. Crumpf cut him short.

"That ghost nonsense? Fairy tales! All ghosts are imaginary!" Then Mr. Crumpf's voice changed and he sounded happy. "Can you make a noise like a ghost?"

Mouseknees was still trembling. "I don't know what kind of noise a ghost makes."

"Just shout, just once. Wait until I tell you. And listen, Mouseknees, I could be very angry at you for sneaking in here tonight but I'll forget it if you'll do me a favor."

"Yes, sir!"

"You come here every evening for the next few nights at this time. Come here in the shed and shout, just once." Then Mr. Crumpf spoke very sternly. "Never let anyone see you. That's important, remember. What would you like to have, Mouseknees, for a gift?"

"Me?" Mouseknees did not have to think twice. "A good collar for my goat."

"All right," said Mr. Crumpf. "Now, listen. In about ten seconds you shout. Then wait here for a few minutes before you go. Then get to the road without anyone seeing you."

"Baah!" said Pahdetoo.

"Goodness, what was that?" Mr. Crumpf jumped. "Keep that goat quiet. Now, ready? Shout!"

Mouseknees shouted. It might have sounded like a ghost but it also sounded partly like a wagon axle, partly like a palm tree rubbing against another palm tree, partly like a fish thrown on dry land, and partly like a small boy, still half scared. And to make it more impressive Pahdetoo added a loud "Baah!"

Mr. Crumpf went to the door. "Now, stay here five minutes, then get away quietly. And come back tomorrow night!" He almost ran from the shed.

Outside Mouseknees could hear people's voices. "What was it? What was it?"

Mr. Crumpf's answer was very clear. "There wasn't a soul around, not a soul. You know, it's strange, but I've heard that cry before. You know, the old superstition—!"

"The ghost?" That was Mrs. Kidley-Plinker. "Oh, dear, I don't feel well. I'll go indoors."

Mr. Crumpf and Mr. Kidley-Plinker were still outside on the lawn and Mouseknees could hear every word.

"My wife is very nervous," the new tenant said.

"I'm so sorry she's upset," Mr. Crumpf answered.

"If this mysterious noise is continued, it will be very bad for her to stay in this house."

"Then I wouldn't think of asking you to stay," Mr. Crumpf said and he sounded pleased. "If you wish, we'll tear up the lease tomorrow."

"You will?" Mr. Kidley-Plinker sounded pleased. "I'll talk to her and see what she thinks."

The men went back to the veranda. Mouseknees took a firm hold on Pahdetoo's rope. "We goin' now. And tomorrow you get a nice collar."

Very carefully he tiptoed from the shed, crossed the side lawn, got around the house. He was safe now. Here were bushes and he could move from one to the other.

He stopped, certain he had heard a noise. It was a noise, the sound of light footsteps. He jumped behind a bush. This was certainly the captain's ghost, for he could see no one. He held tight to Pahdetoo and waited. The steps came nearer. To cry out now would be to disobey Mr. Crumpf's orders and there would be no collar for Pahdetoo. To stay quiet meant that the captain's ghost—!

"Who's there?" It was a woman's voice and Mouseknees took a deep breath. He knew that voice. It was Mrs. Kidley-Plinker.

"Baah!" That was Pahdetoo.

"Come on, come out!" the woman was insistent.

Mouseknees came out.

"Oh, the boy with the goat? Humph! I knew someone was around. Tell me, did you shout just a few minutes ago?"

Mouseknees did not answer.

"I'm sure you did." The woman did not seem angry. "Don't be frightened. I was sure someone was on the place and I just came out to look about. I want you to come here every evening at the same time and shout the same way. Understand? And don't let Mr. Crumpf hear you! I'll talk to you tomorrow at the hotel. Now, run along and don't tell anyone I spoke with you!"

At the hotel the next morning the news went around that the Colonel and his wife had decided to give up Mr. Crumpf's house and to stay at the hotel. Mouseknees said nothing.

That afternoon he was off duty and sitting in the field just behind the garden. Pahdetoo was at his feet, a nice shiny collar on his neck. And Pigeon was there, asking questions.

"You see the ghost?" Pigeon asked for the tenth time.

"Ghosts is all imagination and fairy tales," Mouseknees said solemnly.

"Huh. You didn't say that yesterday."

"Yesterday," Mouseknees said simply, "I didn't know it."

At the edge of the garden stood a woman. It was Mrs. Kidley-Plinker and she was waving.

"What she want me foah?" Pigeon asked.

"She don't," Mouseknees said. "She want me." He went to her.

"There's no need to come tonight," she said mysteriously.

"Yes, ma'am," Mouseknees said. Mr. Crumpf had said the same thing. He took the envelope she handed him. As he walked back to Pigeon he opened it. There was a half dollar inside.

"Lady give me this," Mouseknees said.

"She give it? She give you the goat collar, too?"

"No, she didn't give me that," Mouseknees said and he would say no more for a minute. Then he said, "Ghosts is fairy tales, Pigeon. But a ghost's ghost —that's something else."

"Who ever saw a ghost's ghost?"

Mouseknees smiled and flipped the half dollar in the air and caught it. "Pahdetoo did!"

"Baah!" said Pahdetoo.

The Three Innkeepers
or
The King's Legs

There was once a farmer who got tired of farming, so he thought he would go to the town and start an inn.

But when he got there, he found that there were two inns there already: and one of them was called *The King's Head,* and one was called *The King's Arms.*

"Very well," he said, "I shall call *my* inn *The King's Legs.*"

So he had a beautiful sign painted with the King's

legs on it, and hung up outside.

Now this turned out very well. Nobody had ever heard of an inn being called *The King's Legs* before, so all strangers used to come in out of curiosity, to ask why on earth the inn had got such a strange name. Then, of course, they had at least to buy a drink, and sometimes they stayed the night so as to be able to use note paper with such a lovely address when writing to their friends: and so *The King's Legs* inn became the most prosperous in the town, and the new innkeeper got rich and the old innkeepers began to get poor.

So they put their heads together, and wondered what was the reason. "I know," said the landlord of *The King's Arms*. "It is because he has got such a funny name for his inn. I'm going to change the name of mine."

So he decided to call his inn in future *The King's Stomach*; and he took down the old sign to get a new picture painted. "Mind you make it a big one," he said to the sign-painter, "or else it won't look royal"— though, as a matter of fact, the king of that country was not particularly fat at all.

Then he hung up the new sign and waited to see what happened.

But what happened was not at all what he expected. Some courtiers of the King happened to be travelling that way; and, when they saw the sign, they were very angry and shocked. "What!" they cried: "The impudent creature! Fancy calling *that* great fat stomach the King's! As if everyone didn't know he had the slimmest and most elegant little stomach in the kingdom!"

"What shall we do?" asked one of the courtiers. "Shall we arrest him for high treason and have his head cut off?"

"We might do that," said another of the courtiers. "But, on the whole, wouldn't it be more fun just to throw some stones through his windows?"

The others agreed; so they got off their horses and began throwing stones through the windows of *The King's Stomach* inn until there wasn't a single pane of glass left unbroken. Then they rode on.

So the landlord of *The King's Stomach* said to the landlord of *The King's Head*: "Well, *my* plan didn't work very well. Have *you* got one?"

"Yes, I have," said the landlord of *The King's Head*. "I have thought of a very funny idea." He went and bought a curious sort of gilt bird, and shut it up tight in a glass case, and put a label on it, "Weather cock," and put it in the window of his inn.

Now it wasn't long before some people came by. "Hullo," they said, "that's a funny thing to do, to keep your weather cock shut up in a glass case where the wind can't get at it! I wonder why he does that?"

So they went in to ask.

"Why do you call that funny gold bird in a glass case a 'weather cock'?" they asked, when they had ordered some beer.

"Because," said the landlord, "just what it is, *whether cock* or hen, I can't decide."

Lots of people came in to ask the same question, and he gave them all the same answer.

So now the landlord of the new inn, *The King's Legs,* found all the people going back to *The King's Head,* and himself not getting rich any more.

So he got a large gilt egg, and went along quietly at night, and slipped it in the glass case along with the bird.

Next day some people came by and asked the usual question and were given the usual answer.

"But, you silly old ass!" they cried out to the inn-keeper, "anyone can see it's a hen! Why, it's laid an egg!"

And they were so angry they took up several of the big glass beer tankards that were about and started hitting the landlord with them on the head. It didn't hurt his head much because it was very hard, but it broke all the tankards, and he went along to see his friend about it all.

"It's a funny thing," said his friend, "but whatever

we do it always seems to end in glass being broken."

"That means," said the other one, "there must be some sort of magic in it all."

"Well, in that case," said the first one, "we had better go and see the Village Witch, and ask for her advice."

So they went to the Village Witch, who happened to be also the District Nurse.

"There is only one thing to be done," said the witch. "We must kill him."

"Well, will you do it for us if we pay you?" asked the innkeepers.

"Certainly," said the Witch, and putting on her nurse's uniform she bicycled round to *The King's Legs*. There she found the landlord in the parlor at the back.

"Dear, dear!" she said. "I am sorry to hear you are so ill."

"Am I?" said the landlord. "*I* hadn't heard."

"Perhaps not, but *I* had!" said the witch firmly: "You had better go to bed."

So he went to bed, and she nursed him a bit and then said she would come back the next morning to see how he was.

The next day she came in the morning and went up to his room, looking very sad.

"You can't think," she said, "how sorry I was when I heard you had died in the night."

At that the innkeeper looked very pale and frightened.

"What!" he said. "Died in the night! Are you sure? Nobody told me."

"No," she said firmly; "but they told *me*! I'll send the undertaker round this afternoon to measure you for your coffin."

As it happened the undertaker was busy that afternoon and couldn't come: but he came the next morning.

"Good morning," he said, "I have come to bury you."

"What!" cried the innkeeper, who was just as clever as the witch; "hadn't you heard?"

"Heard what?" said the undertaker.

"Why, I was buried yesterday afternoon! When you didn't come, I got the undertaker from the next town, and *he* buried me."

The undertaker was very sorry at that because he didn't like losing a job, but there was nothing to be done if the innkeeper had been buried already: so he just went away.

Then the innkeeper got up and dressed and went down and started serving drinks in the bar. Pres-

ently the witch and the two other innkeepers looked in, to see if he was safely buried yet.

When they saw him quite well and serving drinks they were very upset.

"Good gracious!" exclaimed the witch, "what are *you* doing here?"

"What!" exclaimed the innkeeper. "But surely you must have heard! I am the new landlord of *The King's Legs*! They buried the last one yesterday afternoon, poor chap!"

At that the two other innkeepers and the witch were so upset that, without saying a word, they all ran hand in hand down the village street to the village pond and drowned themselves there: and the landlord of *The King's Legs* got a small paint-brush and wrote on the bottom of his sign in white paint:

Under Entirely New Management

About Elizabeth Eliza's Piano

Elizabeth Eliza had a present of a piano, and she was to take lessons of the postmaster's daughter.

They decided to have the piano set across the window in the parlor, and the carters brought it in, and went away.

After they had gone the family all came in to look at the piano; but they found the carters had placed it with its back turned towards the middle of the room, standing close against the window.

How could Elizabeth Eliza open it? How could she reach the keys to play upon it?

Solomon John proposed that they should open the window, which Agamemnon could do with his long arms. Then Elizabeth Eliza should go round upon the piazza, and open the piano. Then she could have her music-stool on the piazza, and play upon the piano there.

HENRY C PITZ

So they tried this; and they all thought it was a very pretty sight to see Elizabeth Eliza playing on the piano, while she sat on the piazza, with the honey-suckle vines behind her.

It was very pleasant, too, moonlight evenings. Mr. Peterkin liked to take a doze on his sofa in the room; but the rest of the family liked to sit on the piazza. So did Elizabeth Eliza, only she had to have her back to the moon.

All this did very well through the summer; but, when the fall came, Mr. Peterkin thought the air was too cold from the open window, and the family did not want to sit out on the piazza.

Elizabeth Eliza practised in the mornings with her cloak on; but she was obliged to give up her music in the evenings the family shivered so.

One day, when she was talking with the lady from Philadelphia, she spoke of this trouble.

The lady from Philadelphia looked surprised, and then said, "But why don't you turn the piano round?"

One of the little boys pertly said, "It is a square piano."

But Elizabeth Eliza went home directly, and with the help of Agamemnon and Solomon John, turned the piano round.

"Why did we not think of that before?" said Mrs. Peterkin. "What shall we do when the lady from Philadelphia goes home again?"

The Peterkins Try to Become Wise

They were sitting round the breakfast table, and wondering what they should do because the lady from Philadelphia had gone away. "If," said Mrs. Peterkin, "we could only be more wise as a family!" How could they manage it? Agamemnon had been to college, and the children all went to school; but still as a family they were not wise. "It comes from books,"

[163

and vinegar made very good ink. So they decided to make some. The little boys said they could find some nutgalls up in the woods. So they all agreed to set out and pick some. Mrs. Peterkin put on her cape-bonnet, and the little boys got into their india-rubber boots, and off they went.

The nutgalls were hard to find. There was almost everything else in the woods,—chestnuts and walnuts, and small hazel nuts, and a great many squirrels; and they had to walk a great way before they found any nutgalls. At last they came home with a large basket and two nutgalls in it. Then came the question of the vinegar. Mrs. Peterkin had used her very last on some beets they had the day before. "Suppose we go and ask the minister's wife." said Elizabeth Eliza. So they all went to the minister's wife. She said if they wanted some good vinegar they had better set a barrel of cider down in the cellar, and in a year or two it would make very nice vinegar. But they said they wanted it that very afternoon. When the minister's wife heard this she said she should be very glad to let them have some vinegar, and gave them a cupful to carry home.

So they stirred in the nutgalls, and by the time evening came they had very good ink.

Then Solomon John wanted a pen. Agamemnon had a steel one, but Solomon John said, "Poets always

used quills." Elizabeth Eliza suggested that they
should go out to the poultry yard and get a quill. But
it was already dark. They had, however, two lanterns,
and the little boys borrowed the neighbors'. They set
out in procession for the poultry yard. When they got
there the fowls were all at roost, so they could look
at them quietly. But there were no geese! There were
Shanghais, and Cochin Chinas, and Guinea hens, and
Barbary hens, and speckled hens, and Poland roosters,
and bantams, and ducks, and turkeys, but not one
goose! "No geese but ourselves," said Mrs. Peterkin,
wittily, as they returned to the house. The sight of
this procession roused up the village. "A torchlight
procession!" cried all the boys of the town; and they
gathered round the house, shouting for the flag; and
Mr. Peterkin had to invite them in, and give them
cider and gingerbread, before he could explain to
them that it was only his family visiting his hens.

After the crowd had dispersed Solomon John sat
down to think of his writing again. Agamemnon
agreed to go over to the bookstore to get a quill. They
all went over with him. The bookseller was just shut-
ting up his shop. However, he agreed to go in and get
a quill, which he did, and they hurried home.

So Solomon John sat down again, but there was no
paper. And now the bookstore was shut up. Mr. Peterkin suggested that the mail was about in, and perhaps

he should have a letter, and then they could use the envelope to write upon. So they all went to the post office, and the little boys had their india-rubber boots on, and they all shouted when they found Mr. Peterkin had a letter. The postmaster inquired what they were shouting about; and when they told him he said he would give Solomon John a whole sheet of paper for his book. And they all went back rejoicing.

So Solomon John sat down, and the family all sat round the table looking at him. He had his pen, his ink, and his paper. He dipped his pen into the ink and held it over the paper, and thought a minute, and then said, "But I haven't got anything to say."

Gudbrand on the Hill-side

Once on a time there was a man whose name was
Gudbrand; he had a farm which lay far, far away
upon a hillside, and so they called him Gudbrand on
the Hill-side.

Now, you must know this man and his goodwife
lived so happily together, and understood one another so well, that all the husband did the wife thought
so well done there was nothing like it in the world,
and she was always glad whatever he turned his hand
to. The farm was their own land, and they had a

168]

hundred dollars lying at the bottom of their chest, and two cows tethered up in a stall in their farmyard.

So one day his wife said to Gudbrand:

"Do you know, dear, I think we ought to take one of our cows into town and sell it; that's what I think; for then we shall have some money in hand, and such well-to-do people as we ought to have ready money like the rest of the world. As for the hundred dollars at the bottom of the chest yonder, we can't make a hole in them, and I'm sure I don't know what we want with more than one cow. Besides, we shall gain a little in another way, for then I shall get off with looking after only one cow, instead of having, as now, to feed and litter and water two."

Well, Gudbrand thought his wife talked right good sense, so he set off at once with the cow on his way to town to sell her; but when he got to the town, there was no one who would buy his cow.

"Well! well! never mind," said Gudbrand, "at the worst, I can only go back again with my cow. I've both stable and tether for her, I should think, and the road is no farther out than in"; and with that he began to toddle home with his cow.

But when he had gone a bit of the way, a man met him who had a horse to sell, so Gudbrand thought 'twas better to have a horse than a cow, so he swopped with the man. A little farther on, he met a man walk-

ing along, and driving a fat pig before him, and he
thought it better to have a fat pig than a horse, so he
swopped with the man. After that he went a little
farther, and a man met him with a goat; so he thought
it better to have a goat than a pig, and he swopped
with the man that owned the goat. Then he went on
a bit till he met a man who had a sheep, and he
thought it always better to have a sheep than a goat.
After a while he met a man with a goose, and he
swopped away the sheep for the goose; and when he
had walked a long, long time, he met a man with a
cock, and he swopped with him, for he thought in
this wise, " 'Tis surely better to have a cock than a
goose." Then he went on till the day was far spent,
and he began to get very hungry, so he sold the cock
for a shilling, and bought food with the money, for,
thought Gudbrand on the Hill-side, " 'Tis always
better to save one's life than to have a cock."

After that he went on home till he reached his near-
est neighbor's house, where he turned in.

"Well," said the owner of the house, "how did
things go with you in town?"

"Rather so so," said Gudbrand; "I can't praise my
luck, nor do I blame it either," and with that he told
the whole story from first to last.

"Ah!" said his friend, "you'll get nicely called over
the coals, that one can see, when you get home to

your wife. Heaven help you, I wouldn't stand in your
shoes for something."

"Well!" said Gudbrand on the Hill-side, "I think
things might have gone worse with me; but now,
whether I have done wrong or not, I have so kind a
goodwife, she never has a word to say against anything that I do."

"Oh!" answered his neighbor, "I hear what you
say, but I don't believe it for all that."

"Shall we lay a bet upon it?" asked Gudbrand on
the Hill-side. "I have a hundred dollars at the bottom
of my chest at home; will you lay as many against
them?"

Yes, the friend was ready to bet; so Gudbrand
stayed there till evening, when it began to get dark,
and then they went together to his house, and the
neighbor was to stand outside the door and listen,
while the man went in to see his wife.

"Good evening!" said Gudbrand on the Hill-side.

"Good evening!" said the goodwife. "Oh! is that
you? now, God be praised!"

Yes, it was he. So the wife asked how things had
gone with him in town.

"Oh! only so so," answered Gudbrand; "not much
to brag of. When I got to town there was no one who
would buy the cow, so you must know I swopped it
away for a horse."

"For a horse!" said his wife; "well, that is good of you; thanks with all my heart. We are so well-to-do that we may drive to church, just as well as other people; and if we choose to keep a horse we have a right to get one, I should think. So run out, child, and put up the horse."

"Ah!" said Gudbrand, "but you see I've not got the horse after all; for when I got a bit farther on the road, I swopped it away for a pig."

"Think of that—now!" said the wife; "you did just as I should have done myself; a thousand thanks! Now I can have a bit of bacon in the house to set before people when they come to see me, that I can. What do we want with a horse? People would only say we had got so proud that we couldn't walk to church. Go out, child, and put up the pig in the sty."

"But I've not got the pig either," said Gudbrand; "for when I got a little farther on, I swopped it away for a milch goat."

"Bless us!" cried his wife, "how well you manage everything! Now I think it over, what should I do with a pig? People would only point at us and say, 'Yonder they eat up all they have got.' No! now I have got a goat, and I shall have milk and cheese, and keep the goat too. Run out, child, and put up the goat."

"Nay, but I haven't any goat either," said Gud-brand, "for a little farther on I swopped it away, and got a fine sheep instead."

"You don't say so!" cried his wife; "why, you do everything to please me, just as if I had been with you; what do we want with a goat? If I had it I should lose half my time in climbing up the hills to get it down. No! if I have a sheep, I shall have both wool and clothing, and fresh meat in the house. Run out, child, and put up the sheep."

"But I haven't got the sheep any more than the rest," said Gudbrand, "for when I had gone a bit farther, I swopped it away for a goose."

"Thank you, thank you, with all my heart!" cried his wife; "what should I do with a sheep? I have no spinningwheel, nor carding comb, nor should I care to worry myself with cutting, and shaping, and sew-ing clothes. We can buy clothes now, as we have always done; and now I shall have roast goose, which I have longed for so often; and, besides, down to stuff my little pillow with. Run out, child, and put up the goose."

"Ah!" said Gudbrand, "but I haven't the goose either; for when I had gone a bit farther I swopped it away for a cock."

"Dear me!" cried his wife, "how you think of every-thing! just as I should have done myself! A cock!

think of that! why, it's as good as an eight-day clock, for every morning the cock crows at four o'clock, and we shall be able to stir our stumps in good time. What should we do with a goose? I don't know how to cook it; and as for my pillow, I can stuff it with cotton-grass. Run out, child, and put up the cock."

"But, after all, I haven't got the cock," said Gud-brand; "for when I had gone a bit farther, I got as hungry as a hunter, so I was forced to sell the cock for a shilling, for fear I should starve."

"Now, God be praised that you did so!" cried his wife; "whatever you do, you do it always just after my own heart. What should we do with the cock? We are our own masters, I should think, and can lie abed in the morning as long as we like. Heaven be thanked that I have got you safe back again! you who do everything so well that I want neither cock nor goose; neither pigs nor kine."

Then Gudbrand opened the door and said:

"Well, what do you say now? Have I won the hundred dollars?" and his neighbor was forced to allow that he had.

Rats

Once upon a time there was a man called Smith. He was a greengrocer and lived in Clapham. He had four sons. The eldest was called George, after the king, and it was arranged that he was to inherit his father's shop. So at school he went to special botany classes, and learned about the hundred and fifty-seven different kinds of cabbage, and the forty-four sorts of lettuce. And he went to zoology classes and learned about the seventy-seven kinds of caterpillar that live in cabbages, and how the green kind come out if you sprinkle the cabbages with soapy water, and the striped ones with tobacco juice, and the big fat brown ones with salt water. So when he grew up he was the best greengrocer in London, and no one ever found caterpillars in his cabbages.

But Mr. Smith only had one shop, so his other three sons had to seek their own fortunes. The second son was called Jim, but his real name was James, of course. He went to school and he won all the prizes for English essays. He was captain of the school soccer team, and played halfback. And he was very clever at all sorts of tricks, and used to play them on the masters. One day he stuck a matchhead into the chalk. It wasn't a safety matchhead either, but one of those blue and white ones that strike on anything. So when the master started writing on the board he struck the match, and nobody did much work for the next five minutes. Another day he put methylated spirits in the inkpots, and the ink wouldn't stick to the pens. It took the master half-an-hour to change all the ink, so they didn't get much French done that hour, and he hated French, anyway. But he never did ordinary tricks like putting putty in the keyholes or dead rats in the master's desk.

The third son was called Charles, and he was fairly good at mathematics and history, and got into the cricket eleven as a slow left-handed bowler; but the only thing he was really good at was chemistry. He was the only boy in his school (or in any other, for all I know) who had ever made paradimethylamino-benzaldehyde or even arabitol (which is really quite hard to make, and has nothing to do with rabbits). He could have made the most awful smells if he had wanted to, because he knew how. But he was a good boy and didn't. Besides if he had they might have stopped him doing chemistry, and he wanted to go on doing chemistry all his life.

The fourth son was called Jack. He wasn't much good at any of his lessons, nor at games either. He never managed to kick a ball straight, and he went to sleep when fielding at cricket. The only thing he was any good at was wireless. He made pretty well everything in the set at home, except the valves, and he was learning to make them when the story begins. He had a great-aunt called Matilda who was so old that she said she could remember the railway from London to Dover being built. She couldn't walk, and had to stay in bed all the time. He made her earphones to listen in with, and she said she hadn't been so happy since Queen Victoria's time. Jack was very clever with other electrical things too. He made a special dodge to get electric light for his father's house without paying for it, and the meter didn't register anything for a week. Then his father found out what was happening and said, "We mustn't do that, it's stealing from the electric light company." "I don't think it's stealing," said Jack. "A company isn't a person, and besides the electricity goes through our lamps and back again to the main. So we don't keep it, we only borrow it." But his father made him take his gadget down, and even paid the company for the current, for he was an honest man.

Mr. Smith had a daughter named Lucille, but every one called her Pudgy. She doesn't really come into the story, so I shan't say anything more about her till the end, except that when she was little her front teeth stuck out; but in the end they managed to push them in.

Now at this time there was a great plague of rats in the London Docks. They were specially fierce rats, whose ancestors had come on steamers from Hong Kong along with tea and ginger and silk and rice. These rats ate all sorts of food which are brought to London in ships because we cannot grow enough food in England to feed all the people there. They ate wheat from Canada and cheese from Holland, and mutton from New Zealand and beef from Argentina. They bit out pieces from the middle of Persian carpets to line their nests, and wiped their feet on silk coats from China.

Now the man who is at the head of all the docks in

London is called the Chairman of the Port of London
Authority, and he is a big bug indeed. He has an
office near Tower Hill that is almost as big as Buck·
ingham Palace. He was awfully angry about the rats,
because he has to look after the cargoes that are
brought in ships from the time they are unloaded
till they are taken away in trains and lorries and
carts. So he had to pay for the things the rats ate. He
sent for the best ratcatchers in London. But they only
caught a few hundred rats, because they were a very
cunning kind of rat. They had a king who lived in
a very deep hole, and the other rats brought him spe·
cially good food. They brought him chocolate that
had come from Switzerland, bits of turkey from
France, dates from Algiers, and so on. And he told
the other rats what to do. If any rat got caught in a
trap, he sent out special messengers to give warning
of the danger. He had an army of ten thousand of
the bravest young rats, and they used to fight any
other animals that were sent against them. A terrier
can easily kill one or two rats; but if a hundred rush
at him all at once, he may kill three or four of them,
but the others will kill him in the end. The rats with
the toughest teeth were trained to be engineers, and
used to bite through the wire of rattraps to let pris·
oners out.

So in one month these rats killed a hundred and

eighty-one cats, forty-nine dogs, and ninety-five ferrets. And they wounded a lot of others so badly that
they ran away if they even smelt a rat, let alone saw
one. And they let out seven hundred and forty-two
prisoners from six hundred and eighteen traps. So
the rat-catchers lost their best dogs and ferrets and
traps, and gave up the job in despair. The people in
the docks sent round to the chemists' shops for all
sorts of rat poison, and sprinkled it about mixed with
different sorts of bait. But the king rat gave orders
that none of his subjects were to eat food unless it
came straight out of a box or a barrel or a bag. So
only a few disobedient rats got poisoned, and the
others said it served them right. And the poison was
no more use than the dogs and ferrets and traps.

So the Chairman of the Port of London Authority
called a meeting of the Authority in the great Board
Room of his office, and said, "Can you suggest what
is to be done about the rats?" So the vice-chairman
suggested putting an advertisement in the papers.
The next week advertisements came out in all the
papers. It was on the front page of the ones that have
the news inside, like the *Times* and the *Daily Mail,*
and in the middle of the ones that have the news outside, like the *Daily Herald* and the *Evening Standard.*
It took up a whole page, and was printed in huge letters, so that almost every one in England read it. All

the Smith family read it except great-aunt Matilda,
who never read the papers, because she listened in to
all the broadcast news.

Now this advertisement made all the competitions
in the papers look pretty silly. For the Chairman of
the Port of London Authority offered a hundred
thousand pounds and his only daughter in marriage
to the man who would rid the docks of rats. (If the
winner was married already, of course he wouldn't
be allowed to marry the daughter, but he got a diamond bracelet for his wife as a consolation prize.)
There was a photograph of the hundred thousand
pounds; and they were real golden sovereigns, not
paper notes. And there was a photograph of the
daughter, who was very pretty, with short curly
golden hair and blue eyes. Besides this, she could
play the violin, and had won prizes for cookery, swim-
ming, and figure skating. The only snag was that the
competitors had to bring their own things for killing
the rats, so really it cost a lot of money to go in for
the competition.

Still thousands and thousands of people went in
for it. They had to get three extra postmen to take the
letters to the Chairman the next morning. And so
many people rang him up on the telephone that the
wires melted. For months and months all sorts of
people tried their luck. There were chemists and

magicians, and bacteriologists and sorcerers, and
zoologists and spiritualists and lion hunters, but none
of them were able to kill more than a few rats. What
was worse, they interfered with the unloading of the
ships, and quite a lot of corn had to be sent round by
Liverpool and Cardiff and Hull and Southampton
instead of London.

Among the people who tried their luck were Jim
and Charles and Jack Smith. Jim thought that if only
he could make a trap that looked quite ordinary, he
would be able to fool the rats, just as he used to fool
the masters at school. Now he knew that there were
all sorts of old tins lying about the docks, so he designed a special sort of trap made from an old tin.
The rats smelt the bait inside it and jumped on to
the top. But the top was a trap door, and so the rat
fell through and couldn't get out again. He spent all
his spare time making these traps, and he got his
friend to help. He borrowed ten pounds from his
father, and got Bill Johnson, who was an out-of-work
tinsmith, to make more for him. In the end he had
one thousand three hundred and ninety-four of these
traps; but seventeen of them were pretty bad, so he
didn't bring them.

He went along to Tower Hill with his traps on one
of his father's carts, and saw the vice-chairman, who
was a duke, and was looking after all the ratcatching.

The vice-chairman said, "Of course these traps aren't enough to go all around all the docks, but we will try them on one." So they tried them on the West India Dock, where the ships come from Jamaica and the other islands round it, with sugar and rum and treacle and bananas. I don't think that was a very good place to choose, because the rats there are quite specially quick and nimble. This is because they are constantly tumbling into barrels and vats and hogs-heads and demijohns of treacle. The slow ones get stuck in it, and that is the end of them. Only the quick ones escape. So all the rats round there are very quick, and good climbers.

Half Jim's traps were baited with cheese and half with bacon. The first night they caught nine hundred and eighteen rats. Jim was terribly pleased, and thought he was going to win the prize. But the next night they only caught three rats, and the third only two. The king rat had warned all his subjects to avoid tins, and only stupid or disobedient ones got caught. On the fourth night they moved the traps to the Victoria Docks, but they only caught four rats. The warning had been spread. So Jim went home very sad. He had wasted a lot of time and ten pounds, and the other boys at school called him Tinned Rats.

Charles Smith had quite a different scheme. He invented a special kind of poison with no taste or smell. I am not going to tell you what it was, or how to make it, because some murderer might read this story, and use it to kill all sorts of people. He made a lot of this poison, and he also made a lot of the stuff that gives the smell to Roquefort cheese, which is a very cheesy kind of cheese made in France. This is called methyl-heptadecyl ketone, and I think it has a lovely smell. Some people don't like it, but rats do. He borrowed twenty pounds from his father, and got a hundred cheap and nasty cheeses. Then he cut each into a hundred bits. He soaked them first in the poison, and then in the stuff with the Roquefort smell, and put them into ten thousand cardboard boxes. He thought that if he did that the rats would not think that they were ordinary poisoned bait, which is just scattered about, and not in boxes at all. But the boxes were cardboard, so that the rats could get in quite easily.

All through one day two men with wheelbarrows went round the docks, leaving the ten thousand cheese boxes in different places. And Charles went behind them with a squirt, and squirted the cheesy stuff over them. The whole of East London smelt of cheese that afternoon. When the sun set, the rats came out, and they said to one another, "This must be marvellous cheese, quite a little box of it smells as much as a whole case of ordinary cheeses." So a great

many of them ate it. They even brought some back
to the king rat. But luckily for him he had just had
a huge meal of walnuts and smoked salmon and
wasn't hungry. The poison took some time to work,
and it wasn't until three o'clock in the morning that
the rats began to die of it. The king at once suspected
the cheese, and sent out messengers to warn his subjects against it.

Also there was a wicked rat which had been sen-
tenced to death for eating its own children, and the
king made it eat the bit of cheese that had been
brought him. When it died he knew the cheese was
poisoned, and sent out another lot of messengers. The
next morning they picked up four thousand five hundred and fourteen dead rats, and ever so many more
were dead in their holes, besides others that were ill.
The Chairman was so pleased that he gave Charles
the money to buy another lot of cheeses. But when,
two days later, they left them about, only two out of
eight thousand boxes had been opened. So they knew
the rats had been too clever for them again. Charles
was very sad indeed. He had been so sure of success
that he had ordered a wedding ring for his marriage
with the Chairman's daughter, and written to the
Archbishop of Canterbury to marry them. Now he
had to write to the jeweller and the Archbishop to
say he wasn't going to marry after all. And worst of

all, the cheesy smell stuck to him for a month. They wouldn't have him back at school, and he had to sleep in the coal shed at home.

Last of all Jack tried his plan. It needed a lot of money, and though he borrowed thirty pounds from his father, it was not enough. But he borrowed some from me, and sold some wireless sets that he had made, until he gradually got all he needed. He bought some very fine iron filings, much finer than the ordinary kind, and had them baked into biscuits. The biscuits were left about the docks. At first the rats would not touch them, but later they found they did them no harm, and began to eat them. Meanwhile Jack got seven perfectly enormous electro-magnets, which were put in different docks. Each was in the middle of a deep pit with smooth sides. And cables were laid so that current from the District Railway and the East London Railway could be put through the magnets. Luckily Jack knew the head electrical engineer on the underground railways, because they were both keen on wireless, so he was able to arrange to borrow their current. When he thought that the rats had eaten enough iron filings he made arrangements to turn the current through the magnets. All loose iron, steel, or nickel things had to be tied up very tight indeed with extra cables. And all the people in the docks that night had to wear special boots or shoes with no nails in them; except the vice-chairman who was a duke, so of course he had gold nails in his boots.

At half past one in the morning the last underground railway train had stopped, and they turned all the current that had been working the trains into the first magnet. A few rusty nails and tin cans came rushing towards it, and so did the rats, but more slowly. They were full of iron filings, and the magnet just pulled them. Soon the hole round that magnet was full of rats, and they switched the current on to the next magnet. Then they turned on the third magnet, and so on. Of course only the rats that were above ground were pulled into the holes by the magnets. But they turned them on again and again, and as more and more came out of their holes they were caught too.

The king rat knew something was going wrong, and felt himself pulled to one side of his hole. He sent out messengers but they never came back. At last he went out himself, and a magnet pulled him into one of the pits. When morning came they turned on water taps and drowned all the rats that had been caught by the magnets. These rats weighed a hundred and fifty tons. No one ever counted them, but they reckoned to have caught three-quarters of a million.

There were some awkward accidents. A night-watchman called Alf Timmins had forgotten to wear boots without nails. So the magnet pulled him along feet first. He managed to get his boots off just as he was on the edge of the rat pit, but a rat hung on to each of his toes, and the magnet pulled these rats so hard that all his toes came off. So now he has no toes, like the Pobble, and takes a smaller size in boots than he used to. But another watchman called Bert Higgs had better luck. Before the war he had been a great billiard player, but he got a bit of a shell into his brain, and couldn't play billiards any more. And none of the doctors could get the bit out. So when Jack turned the magnet on the bit of shell came popping out of his head, and the part of his brain that made him so good at billiards started working again. So now he is billiard champion of Poplar.

The next night they turned on the magnets again, and caught a lot more rats, about a hundred tons. Their king was dead, so they did not know what to do. The third night they caught a lot more again. After that the few rats that were left were so frightened that they all ran away. Some went into London, and were a great nuisance to the people there, but none stayed in the docks. They caught none the fourth night, and though they hunted with dogs and ferrets the next day, there wasn't a rat in the place.

So Jack Smith got the hundred thousand pounds and married the Chairman's daughter on a ship at sea. He didn't want to be married in church, and he thought registrar's offices were ugly, so he hired a ship, and when they were three miles from shore the captain married them, which he couldn't have done if they had been only two and a half miles away, because that is the law. They had two boys and two girls, and Jack got a very good job with the B. B. C. as an engineer. With all that money he might have lived all his life without doing any work, but he was so fond of wireless that he wanted to go on working at it.

His sister married the duke, so she is a duchess; but of course duchesses aren't so important now as they used to be. She has diamond heels to her shoes to match her husband's gold nails. He gave his brothers Jim and Charles money to start in their professions. So Jim spent it on magic wands and trick hats and tables, and became a conjuror, and a very good one too. And Charles went to the University and became a professor of chemistry. I am a professor too, and I know him quite well. So they all lived happily ever after.

The Palace on the Rock

There was once a King who lived in a one-roomed palace. It was on the top of a steep rock right in the middle of the town he governed. The top of the rock was so small that the palace covered it all, though the palace had only one room; and the sides of the rock were so steep that the only way to get up to the palace was to climb a rope.

192]

Now this was all very well when the King was young; but as he got older he and the Queen had more and more children; and so, living together in one room like that, they began to feel rather crowded. The Queen was always telling the King he ought to build on other rooms to the palace. But when she said that the King always asked her what she thought he was to build them on, seeing the palace already covered the whole of the rock.

But all the same the King thought there must be some way of doing it, so he sent for his Prime Minister. The Prime Minister was an old man with a long white beard, and did not much like scrambling up a rope to the palace, but when the King told him to, he had to, of course. So up he came.

"Look!" said the King, "I've got sixteen children, and the Queen and I and all sixteen have to live together in one room. Just look what it's like!"

And indeed the room was in a terrible mess. The King sat on his throne in the middle with two of the older boys running clockwork trains between his legs. One of the little princesses was sitting in the coal-scuttle because there were no empty chairs left to sit on. The Queen had cleverly sewn the bottoms of two of the curtains to the tops, in order to make bags, and two more children were sitting in them. The eldest prince shot at them with a water pistol if they put

HENRY C PITZ

their heads out. Two other children had climbed on to the King's desk and were busy emptying his inkpot into the milk jug. Far more children were sitting on the Queen's knees than there was room for, and the youngest of all, the baby, was asleep in the King's crown, which had been hung upside down from a hook in the ceiling.

The Prime Minister looked, and he agreed that something would have to be done about it; but the difficulty was to know what. So he told the King he would think it over.

"All right," said the King, "but think it over fairly quickly; and if you haven't thought what is to be done in a week it will be the worse for you."

So the Prime Minister slid down the rope again, and began to think. But he couldn't think of anything. Then he remembered he had heard that down by the seaside a long way off there lived a wise old man. And he thought perhaps that wise old man could help him. So the Prime Minister took his bicycle and began to bicycle to the sea. It was a long way, and there were many hills to go up and many hills to go down, and he was tired and out of breath when at last he came to the seaside.

There by the sea sat an old man mending some very large lobster pots (which are traps for catching lobsters in). The old man did not look very wise, but the Prime Minister told him what the trouble was, and asked him what to do.

"How much money have you got with you?" said the old man.

"I've got sixteen pounds," said the Prime Minister.

"That will be just enough," said the old man, "to buy from me these sixteen lobster pots. And if you buy them I will give you sixteen big iron hooks as a present."

"Why should I want your lobster pots?" said the Prime Minister crossly. "What use are they to me?"

"Think!" said the old man. "After all, you *are* Prime Minister, you ought to be able to think out a simple thing like that! How many windows has the one-roomed palace got?"

"Sixteen," said the Prime Minister.

"Well, then," said the old man, "that is just right. Hurry up, pay your money and take them away."

So the Prime Minister paid for the pots and tied them all over his bicycle. Then he hung the iron hooks round his neck where they dangled and jangled, and started to ride back to the town. It had been difficult enough riding down to the sea, and it was far harder and more tiring riding back to the town with all those pots and iron hooks. The Prime Minister was tired and dusty and thirsty and wanting tea and buttered toast more than ever he had in his life before, when at last he got back to his home. But all the same he only made a hurried tea, and then climbed up the rope to the palace with all his pots and hooks.

When he got there, things were worse than ever before. If the children had been naughty before they were twice as naughty now, and the King and Queen were nearly distracted.

"If you have got a really good idea," said the King, "I will give you ten sacks full of treasure."

"Right," said the Prime Minister, "I have." And he put all the pots down on the floor. He then put a bag of candy in each pot. Then he went away as if he had forgotten the pots and began leaning out of the windows, fixing an iron hook outside to the windowsill of each one.

Now it was not long before the children caught sight of the candy in the lobster pots, because lobster pots are made of a sort of open basketwork that you can easily see into. Each lobster pot has a hole, of course, for the lobster to get in by. And once they saw the candy inside it was not long before the children were wriggling through the holes after it, one into each pot. Now, though lobster pots are easy to get into, the whole cleverness in making them lies in the fact that they are not nearly so easy to get out of. Once the children were inside them, there they were. They squawked a little and asked to be taken out.

"Not a bit of it," said the Prime Minister. "That's where you stay!" And taking all the lobster pots one by one he hung them on the hooks outside each of the windows.

"There!" he said to the King and Queen. "Now you can have the whole room to yourselves, and a little peace at last! And yet the children will be quite handy to give their suppers to—if you remember to give them suppers, that is to say.

"If they squawk too much you can just shut the windows," he added.

The King and Queen were delighted, and thought they had the cleverest Prime Minister that any King ever had (and indeed there are not many prime ministers today who can manage the same trouble so neatly). So the King gave him his sacks of treasure gladly, and the Prime Minister went home to have a second tea; and as he was eating it he looked out of his own window up at the palace, and thought how pretty the lobster pots looked, swinging from all the windowsills, each with one of the pretty little royal children inside it.

Juan Cigarron

[Which means, in English, Johnny Cigar]

Once there was and was not a poor couple who had many children. The eldest was a clever rascal, always plaguing the younger ones, always turning a trick to benefit himself. At last when the thirteenth child was born, the father said to the eldest, "Juan Cigarron, you are a clever rascal. You can do your own whistling. Go and seek your fortune. There is no longer enough in the house to eat."

So into God's world went Juan Cigarron. As he followed this road and that he said to himself, "I am such a good rascal, I will make a better wizard." So

200]

he served as an apprentice to all the wizards in Spain until he could beat them all at their game. He bore himself like one who consorted with magic. He fooled the world to perfection. Everybody believed in him because everybody wanted to believe in him; and so he became famous.

Now, it happened one day in the King's palace that all the silver plate disappeared. One day it was there and the King was eating from it, just as he had eaten from it every day. The next day, the silver was gone—plates, goblets, trenches, and tankards—as if the earth had swallowed them.

"Send for Juan Cigarron," said the King. "I have heard that he is the greatest wizard in Spain. I believe that he may be the greatest rascal. We will try him."

So a messenger was sent and Juan Cigarron was brought to the palace, straight to the hall where the King sat eating from a common clay dish.

"The royal silver is gone—stolen. You are to discover it, and who stole it," said the King. "But you will make your discovery locked in the deepest dungeon in the palace. Being a great wizard you can manage there as well as anywhere else to find it. If you should turn out to be a cheating rascal instead of a wizard, we will have you there safe, hide and hair, to hang as a fine example. Three days you shall have to find the royal silver."

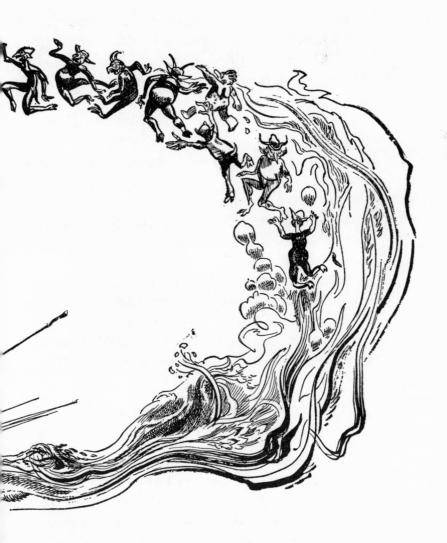

Henry C. Pitz.

The guards led Juan Cigarron to the dungeon.
They fastened an iron ball and chain to his feet. They
locked him in with a key as large as his thigh bone.
They left him alone all day that he might better practice his magic, and all day his heart grew heavier.

"I am well caught," thought Juan Cigarron to himself. "There never was a wizard who died comfortably in his bed. Already, I feel a hempen collar about
my throat. Ah me!"

At the end of the day there came one of the King's
pages to bring him food. In despair Juan Cigarron
watched the jailor unlock the door for him to enter.
He watched the page place the food on the bench before him, and watched him turn away. All the time
he was thinking, "I have paid dearly for my whistle.
Three days of life granted me—no more, no less—and
already one is completed." And he groaned aloud as
the jailor unlocked the door for the page to go his
way.

> "Ay, by San Bruno, this is no fun;
> Of the three—there goes one!"

Whereupon, hearing those words, the page took to
his heels and ran as if the devil himself were after
him. Finding the King's two other pages waiting for
him in a corner of the palace wall, he told them
breathlessly what Juan Cigarron had said. "Not a

doubt of it. He is the greatest wizard on earth. He knows we three have stolen the silver and buried it in the graveyard. We are wholly undone. Let us go to him and confess."

"Never," said one of the others. "You are a weakling. Your ears did not hear right. Tomorrow I will carry his supper to him and then we shall see."

At the end of the second day the heart of Juan Cigarron had become as heavy as the irons on his feet. With what agony did he watch the second page enter his dungeon, leave his food, and depart. Counting off another day of life he groaned aloud:

> "Now, by San José, honest and true,
> Of the three—I've counted two."

If one devil had been at the heels of the first page, a score were hounding the second. "He knows—he knows!" he screamed to the two waiting for him. "We are lost."

"Not yet," said the third and oldest page. "We wait. I myself will carry his supper tomorrow night. I shall not run from the cell. I shall stand beside him and mark his words with care."

At the end of the third day, so tightly could he feel the rope drawn about his neck, Juan Cigarron could not eat his supper for choking. Looking up from his bench and seeing the third page still at his elbow he thought—"Here is a lad who feels pity for me." And aloud he said:

> "Good San Andras, counsel me.
> They've come and gone—all three!"

The page threw himself at the jailed feet of Juan Cigarron. He groveled there. "Master wizard, pity us! Have compassion. Do not tell the King that it is his three pages who have stolen the silver. We will have our necks wrung tomorrow like so many cockerels if you do. Spare us and we will tell you where it lies buried and never, never again, will we commit such an indiscretion."

With great dignity Juan Cigarron rose to his feet. "Do you not know that young rascals have a way of turning into old rascals? How do I know that by saving your necks now I shall not be sending you to purgatory later with more sins to atone for! Enough groveling. I will pardon you this time. But you must swear by all the saints never to steal again—not so much as an *ochavito*. Tomorrow when I appear before the King, bring the silver in secret to the dungeon here, every last piece of it."

So on the morrow Juan Cigarron was not hung. He told the King where the silver plate would be found; and there it was, sure enough. The King was more

pleased than nothing. He embraced Juan Cigarron
and kissed him on both cheeks.

"I did you a great wrong, but I will make restitu-
tion. From now on you shall be, not a wizard to all
the world, but my own particular, royal wizard. You
shall live with me always, in the palace, where you
will be handy to turn a trick of magic when the occa-
sion arises. You are great . . . stupendous . . . more
magnificent than all the wizards," and he embraced
him again.

So Juan Cigarron lived in the palace, eating with
the King, sleeping in his antechamber, going where
the King went; and growing thinner and paler and
more dejected every day. "What will I do when the
next calamity falls! Ah me!" groaned Juan Cigarron,
as each new hour in the day struck.

At last there came an evening when the King happened to be walking alone in his garden. He was
smoking and thinking that it was time Juan Cigarron
should have his wits and his magic put to the test
again. Thinking to practice a clever trick on him, the
King took from his mouth the cigar and from his
pocket his wallet. Into the wallet he stuffed his cigar;
and back into his pocket went both of them. Then
he sent a page for the wizard.

When Juan Cigarron stood before him, the King
put him this question: "What did I have in my mind

that I took out of my mouth and put for safe keeping
in my wallet?" Meaning that he had been thinking
of Cigarron, smoking cigarron and had put cigarron
in his pocket.

But Juan Cigarron was in terror of his life. Here
was the moment of his doom descending upon him.
Hardly knowing that he spoke he muttered, more to
himself than to the King,

> "What a fool is man to pretend—
> Poor Juan Cigarron has met a bad end!"

How the King did laugh at that. He clapped his
hand to his pocket, drew out the wallet and showed
the cigar snuffed out, quite dead. Casting it from him,
he embraced Juan Cigarron for a third time and said,
"That was as clever an answer as ever I heard. I will
grant for that, any wish that is yours to make."

"Any wish?" asked Juan Cigarron.

"Any wish," confirmed the King.

"Then I wish to end my days as a wizard tonight—
and begin them tomorrow as a simple man."

Ebenezer
Never-Could-Sneezer

Ebenezer Never-Could-Sneezer was a wonderful old
French soldier. Years long gone he had been retired

from Napoleon's army with a pension of one cheese a week for as long as he lived. He was a great favorite with the children in his village. He could do *anything*. He could tell stories by the hour. He never seemed to begin a story. He never seemed to end a story. But he could tell them all the same. All the children loved to listen. He told them stories of little boys and girls he had seen when he had been a soldier in Napoleon's armies: little boys and girls in Spain; little boys and girls in Italy; little boys and girls in Austria; little boys and girls in Egypt; little boys and girls in Russia.

But in spite of the fact that Ebenezer could do *anything*, and tell stories by the hour, there was one thing he could not do. He simply could not sneeze. You might suppose it was because he never caught cold. But no, it wasn't that. He sometimes did catch cold. You might suppose it was because he never shook pepper in his soup. But no, it wasn't that. He sometimes did shake pepper in his soup. The reason he couldn't sneeze was because he had no nose to sneeze with. What! No nose! Oh dear, how did that happen?

Ebenezer had a nose when he was a baby. He had a nose when he was a small boy. He had a nose when he was a young man. He had a nose when he marched away with Napoleon's army to fight for France. He

had a nose before the battle of Austerlitz. But after
the battle of Austerlitz his nose was gone. A cannon
ball tweaked it off and took it away. And that's why
he never could sneeze. It wasn't because he never
caught cold. It wasn't because he never shook pepper
in his soup. It was because he had no nose to sneeze
with.

Now the strangest part was that sometimes Ebenezer wanted to sneeze very badly. Though his nose
had been tweaked off by a cannon ball, still, sometimes, he could feel his nose itching. And, oh, how
he wanted to sneeze. He could throw back his head,
open his mouth, close his eyes and say, "Ah—ah—
ah—," or he could say, "Ker—ker—ker," just as well
as you or anyone else. But he could not say a single,
"Choo!" Just imagine getting ready to say a good,
satisfying, "Choo!" and then not being able to say it.
It was dreadful.

One morning Ebenezer had what he thought was
a very brilliant idea. He would make himself a
wooden nose. In the woodpile he found just the piece
of wood he needed. With his pocket knife he whittled
out a nose in wood that looked very much like the
nose he had before the battle of Austerlitz. It was a
very large nose, but that suited Ebenezer's purpose
so much the better. In the end of it where the nos-
trils would naturally be, he bored a hole as large as

the mouth of a bottle. Into this hole he fitted a cork-stopper just as you would in a bottle. He fastened his wooden nose in place with glue, put a cork-screw in one of his pockets and sat down in the sun to wait until he should feel like sneezing.

Presently, sure enough, Ebenezer felt a sneeze coming and trembled all over with excitement. Soon he would know whether his new wooden nose were a success or a failure. Hopefully he threw back his head, opened his mouth, closed his eyes and said, "Ah—ah—ah—!" Oh dear, oh dear, where had he put that cork-screw? In which pocket was it hiding? As fast as his fingers could fly he hunted in his coat pockets. The cork-screw wasn't there. And all the time he kept saying, "Ah—ah—ah—!" Then he hunted in his vest pockets. The day was saved. There was the cork-screw. Fast as he could, he screwed it into the cork-stopper in the end of his nose, and just at the end of another, "Ah—ah—ah—," he gave it a quick pull and out it came with a loud, "Pop!"

He tried it again. "Ah—ah—ah—POP!" "Ker—ker—ker—POP!" Well, that was something. But after all, it was a disappointment. He couldn't really feel satisfied with an "Ah—ah—ah—POP!" or a "Ker—ker—ker—POP!" when what he wanted with all his heart was a good loud, "Ah—ah—ah—CHOO!" or a "Ker—ker—ker—CHOO!" "I am afraid," he said to himself

in despair, "that I shall never, never sneeze again."
So he threw away the cork-screw. He threw away the
cork-stopper. And he threw away the wooden nose.

But even at that moment of his greatest disappointment, affairs were shaping in the world outside his village that were going to bring Ebenezer a very happy
surprise. There came a rumor that the new railroad
from Paris to the sea would run right smack through
the village. With a yawn and a stretch the sleepy little
town woke up and began to buzz with talk. "A railroad! What do you think of that!" said everybody to
everybody else. "We'll have a station, too," they said,
"where trains will arrive and depart just as they do
in Paris." So it went. Buzz, buzz, buzz; how their
tongues ran on. The more they talked of the railroad,
the more excited they became. The Town Fathers
renamed the streets for famous boulevards of Paris.
The Mayor began to carry a cane and wear a silk hat.
The Jack-of-all-trades mended the clock in the town
hall steeple, and for the first time in half a century
people could tell what time it was once more.

For months the rumors flew. For months the rumors were confirmed. For months they worked on
plans. For months they worked on the tracks. For
months they worked on the station. Until finally the
day of the first train arrived. No one in the village
had ever seen a railroad train, or a railroad engine, so

they made a gala day of it and flocked to the station. And of course Ebenezer was there, too.

The new station shone like a dandelion in its fresh coat of yellow paint. The new tracks disappeared in one direction toward Paris and in the other direction toward the sea. The people were so excited that half of them were talking and half of them were laughing. Then the half that had been talking began to laugh and the half that had been laughing began to talk, until they were so mixed up that every one was talking out of one side of his mouth and laughing out of the other side of his mouth at the same time. You never heard such a bedlam! In the midst of it the town hall clock struck eleven. The train was due.

"H-ooooooo—h-ooooooooo—hoo-hoo!" Right on the dot the train whistled. Right on the dot it appeared in sight. Right on the dot it drew up at the station, bell ringing, steam escaping, engine panting, brakes grinding. Everybody shouted. Babies screamed and dogs barked. People waved from the windows of the train. People waved from everywhere on the station platform. Ebenezer waved both hands at once. "Rat-tat-tat" down the steps of the car came the Conductor's heels with the Conductor after them, throwing out his swelling chest as he came. He bowed. He beamed. He strutted. He shook hands with the Station Agent. He shook hands with the Mayor. He shook hands with the Mayor's new cane. He shook hands with everybody, including Ebenezer, until it was time for the train to depart.

Oh, that was a big moment for Ebenezer! Just as the Conductor shouted "A-llllll aboard!", just as the engine bell began to ring, just as the Engineer put his hand on the throttle, Ebenezer felt a sneeze coming. Back flew his head. Open flew his mouth. Tight shut his eyes. "Ah—ah—ah—," said Ebenezer. "CHOO!" said the engine. "Ker—ker—ker—," said Ebenezer. "CHOO!" said the engine. Oh it was a great big whacker of a choo, a delicious choo, the noisiest, juiciest CHOO you ever heard. "Ah—ah—ah—CHOO!" Ker—ker—ker—CHOO!" The first good, satisfying sneeze Ebenezer had had since before the battle of Austerlitz! He kept it up as long as the train was in sight.

From that day on, Ebenezer saved all his sneezes for train time. He knew when every train would depart and never missed a train. He would wait until the Conductor called, "A-llllll aboard!" He would wait until the engine bell rang and the Engineer put his hand on the throttle. Then he would throw back his head, open his mouth, shut his eyes and say, "Ah—ah—ah—" and "CHOO" would say the engine. "Ker—ker—ker—," he would say. "CHOO!" would say the engine. Ah—ah—ah—choo—choo! Ker—ker—ker—choo—choo! Ah·

ah-ker-choo-choo-choo! Ah-ker-choo-choo-choo! Ah-ker-choo-choo! Ah-ker-choo! Ah-ker-choo! Ah-ker-choo! Ahkerchoo, ahkerchoo, ahkerchoo-ahkerchoo-ahkerchoo-ahkerchoo!

There, now if you have your breath again after all that sneezing, here's the end of it. To this very day when the little boys and girls in that village hear the trains leaving the station, they laugh and say, "There goes Ebenezer-Never-Could-Sneezer's Nose."

The Wee Red Man

'Twas in the faraway of long ago, when the world was rare and happenin's quarer, a thousand times than they are today, that this befell.

'Twas in Donegal there fought and wrought against Fate, the world, and the divil, one Conal O'Donnell, a blacksmith by trade, and as honest and kindly a craiture as the dogs ever barked at. But after a wrastle and a tussle, that lasted for years, the world and the divil got the better of Conal, and laid him out flat as a pancake, an' as poor as a Feb'uary snipe. There was one morning at last, he got up out of his bed, without the makin's of a meal in the house, his mealchest as empty as a school on Sunday, no morsel in the cupboard, and his pocket without power to produce a jingle, though he should dance the Highland-fling.

Downhearted he walked out of his house and stood him at the door of his blacksmith's forge, adjoinin', with his shoulder against the jamb of the door, his arms crossed, and his eyes and his heart at his feet, both of them. When all at once he heard a clatter of a horse, and liftin' his eyes, he beheld, ridin' up the road, a little red man upon a little pony.

The Little Red Man drew in with a "God save ye, Conal O'Donnell!"

"Save yourself," says Conal, givin' back the courtesy. "Is it anything I can do for you?"

"Would you lend me," says the Little Red Man, "the loan of your forge fire for a wheen o' minutes till I shoe my horse?"

"With a heart and a half," says Conal O'Donnell, who was always the heart and soul of a good fellow.

"And would you lend me," says the Little Red Man, "the loan of a carvin' knife?"

Now Conal O'Donnell, in all his born days, had never before heard of a horse being shod with a carvin' knife. But he was too polite to question a stranger; so a carvin' knife he fetched in a jiffy. Then on a big stone, that stood by the forge door, the Little Red Man sharpened his carvin' knife, sharpened it up, and sharpened it up, and sharpened it up, till he could only afford to finger the edge very jinteely. Then the Little Red Man went over to his pony, cut the four legs off him at the knees, gathered them up in his arms, and stuck them into the forge fire, and covered them up with coals.

"Conal O'Donnell," says the Little Red Fellow, "could you kindly blow the bellows for me?"

Now Conal was all dumbfoundered at this new way of shoeing a horse. But he was too polite to question a stranger. So the bellows he blew and blew, workin' them like a Connaughtman, and sending up the flames like a fury.

And when at length he thought the four legs must be burned to a cinder, the Little Red Fellow says, "I think they're done, now."

And goin' over to the fire, and rakin' the coals aside, he lifts out in his arms, lo and behold ye, four new legs with a new set of shoes on the ends of them—goes out and sticks the four legs under the pony, and jumpin' on the pony's back, says, "Goodmornin' to ye, thank ye, and good luck to ye, Conal O'Donnell!" and rides off.

Poor Conal, all dumbfoundered, stood like a stone statue in his forge door, lookin' after the Little Red Fellow, and when his speeches returned to him, "Well, that's the wonderfullest way," says he, "and the convenientest that I ever heard tell, of shoeing a horse. It's wish I do that I had known that way thirty years ago, and 'tis the rich man I'd now be entirely."

The words weren't well out of Conal when, behold ye, he heard the clatter of a horse again, and lookin' down the road, who should he see come ridin' up but the King of Ireland himself, upon a beautiful dancin', prancin', yellow steed.

And when the King of Ireland got as far as the forge, he reined in his beautiful, dancin', prancin', yellow steed and says, "Good mornin', Conal O'Don-nell!"

"Good mornin', King of Ireland!" says Conal, says he. "Is it anythin' I can do for ye?"

"Ye can shoe my horse for me," says the King of Ireland, jumpin' off his steed, and throwin' the reins to Conal, "and I'll be forever grateful. And while you're shoein' him I think I'll take a wander up the hill here, and look around upon my kingdom, to see if it is all there, yet. Take good care of my steed," says he, "because he's the valubelest in Ireland, and you might leg it all the way to Australia and home again, without meetin' up with his likes."

"The best of care he'll get at my hands," says Conal, says he, leadin' him into the forge, as the King went strollin' up the hill.

Then Conal went out to the house to look for a

carvin' knife—to try the new way of shoeing a horse.
Upon a stone by the forge door he sharpened the
carvin' knife till he had a jinteel edge upon it, then
makin' up to the King of Ireland's beautiful dancin',
prancin', yellow steed he cut the four legs off him at
the knees, and slipped them into the forge fire, and
covered them up with coals. To the bellows then he
went, and worked them like a Connaughtman, while
the flames went up like fury. And when at length he
thought they were done, he went to the fire, and
raked the coals aside, there wasn't anything left there
but cinders.

Through the forge door he beheld the King of
Ireland comin' down the hill again to get his beautiful dancin', prancin', yellow steed, which was now
lying there with divil a leg to him.

"Och, och," says Conal, says he, throwin' up his
hands, " 'tis behead me the King of Ireland'll do for
slayin' his beautiful steed!" And jumpin' out of the
back window, he ran for the woods.

When the King of Ireland entered the forge, and
beheld the spectacle that met his astonished eyes, he
began dancin' like a madman.

But before many hours he had the whole of his
army and half of his butlers screening the country, to
fetch him Conal O'Donnell, dead or alive.

Three days and three nights they searched, without

MENRU C PITZ.

findin' him, and then give it up. On the fourth night
poor Conal returned home, and slept there that night.
And early the next mornin' he was out of his bed,
heavy-eyed and down-hearted. And wanderin' out of
his door, he stood in the door of his forge, with arms
crossed and shoulders leant against the jamb of the
door, lookin' dejectedly at the ground.

When all at once he heard the clatter of a horse
again on the road. And liftin' his eyes, and lookin'
down the road, what did he behold but the Wee Red
Man again comin' up ridin' upon his pony. But Conal
saw this mornin' the Wee Red Fellow had two others,
one ridin' before him and one behind him—two of
the ugliest old hags that had ever hurt the sight of
Conal in his life long.

And when the Wee Red Fellow, between the two
beauties, drew up at the forge and said, "Good mornin', Conal O'Donnell," 'tis gruff enough Conal answered, "Good mornin'."

"Conal O'Donnell," says the Wee Red Man,
"would you lend me the loan of your forge fire for
a few minutes, this mornin'?"

And Conal, who was always the heart and soul of
a good fellow, never could deny nothing to nobody,
answered him, "Yes, with a heart and a half, you can
have the loan of my forge fire."

And Conal stood aside to see what trick the Wee

Red Fellow was up to this mornin'.

The lad jumped off his pony, and takin' hold of the two ugly old hags, in his arms, he lifted them off, and carried them into the forge, and stuck them into the forge fire, and covered them up with coals. And, "Conal O'Donnell," says he, "would you kindly blow the bellows for me?"

Now Conal O'Donnell was all dumbfounded. But he was too polite to question a stranger. So the bellows he worked like a Connaughtman, and the flames went up like fury. And when at length Conal O'Donnell considered that the two old hags must be burnt to a cinder, the Little Red Man says, "I think they're done, now."

And goin' to the fire, and rakin' the coals aside, behold ye, the Little Red Fellow lifted out of the fire the most beautiful young maiden that Conal had ever beheld in all his born days—carried her out and saited her on the pony, jumped up behind, and said, "Good mornin', good luck to ye, and thank ye, Conal O'Donnell!" and rode off.

All dumbfounded, Conal stood in his forge door, lookin' after the disappearing pair. And when his speeches come to him, says he to himself, "Well, that's the wonderfullest and the convenientest way that I ever heard tell of turnin' ugly old hags into beautiful young maidens. Now," says Conal, says he, "I

have an ugly old wife and an ugly old mother-in-law
in the house here, and from cock-crow to candlelight
the sorra a thing they do but jarrin' and jibin', squabblin' and scoldin', and when the two of them aren't
scoldin' one another, both of them are scoldin' me.
Now," says he, "wouldn't it be a fine thing entirely
if I could only get a beautiful young maiden out of
the pair of them."

Without any more ado, into the house he went, and
there he saw his ugly old wife, at one side of the fire.
and his ugly old mother-in-law, on the other side of
the fire, and they were jarrin' and squabblin', and
scoldin', and both of them spittin' at each other across
the fire.

"Well, by this and by that," says Conal, says he,
stampin' his foot in the middle of the floor, "but I'll
soon and sudden put an end to this!"

And running at them he got hold of the pair in
his arms, and carried them out, screamin' and yellin'
and howlin' and kickin', and kickin' and kickin'! and
stuck the both of them into the forge fire, and covered them up with coals. Then to the bellows he went,
and worked like a Connaughtman, and the flames
come up like furies, around the old women. And
when at length Conal considered that they were done,
he went to the fire, brushed the coals aside, and, lo

and behold ye, they were both done—brown—burnt to two cinders in the fire.

Poor Conal threw up his hands, shoutin', "Now my life is lost, entirely. The King of Ireland'll behead me for killin' his horse, and, after, they'll hang me for murderin' my wife and my mother-in-law!"

Out of the back window he jumped, and away to the woods. He ran three days and three nights, without stoppin', and on the fourth day, tired and hungry, he sat down beside a stream of water and took out of his pocket the last bit of bread he had in the world to eat.

But just that instant Conal heard a piteous voice at his elbow say, "Conal O'Donnell, I'm very hungry. Will you divide with me?" And lookin' around, who should he see, at his shoulder, but the Wee Red Man.

Little as was the love that Conal owed the Little Red Man, the moment he saw the hungry look in the little fellow's eyes, Conal broke his bread in two, and gave half of it to his enemy.

The Wee Red Fellow clapped his hands, sayin', "Why, Conal O'Donnell, you're the best hearted man in all the world, and I'd like to help you."

"Help me," says Conal, "help me. You have helped me, sure enough, and 'tis no more of your kind of help I'm hungerin' for. Begone from my sight!"

"Oh, but, Conal," says the Little Red Fellow, "I'm goin' to help you now in real earnest. Wherever you go I'll go with you as your servant-boy. And I assure you, you'll win fame and fortune."

But no, no, no, Conal protested that he wouldn't have the Wee Red Fellow around him, if he was paved with golden guineas from the crown of his head to the sole of his foot. But 'twas all no use; the Little Red Fellow insisted and persisted so, that Conal at length, in order to get rid of him, had to let him come with him.

Off, then, they started upon their travels, and at a point where the road was crossin' a high hill, they saw a post standin' up with a placard on it. And when they read it, what the placard said was that the King of France was dyin', and all the greatest doctors in the world had tried to cure him, but had failed. And the Queen of France was now offerin' five bags of gold to any doctor in all the world who would cure the King.

The Little Red Man he shouted for joy. "Now, Conal," says he, "your fortune is made. It's go to France you'll do, and cure the King, and get five bags of gold."

"Is it me," says Conal, says he, "to cure the King? Why, I couldn't cure a calf, let alone a king."

"Oh, but," says the Little Red Man, "when I'm with you, there's nothin' in the world we can't do."

And the Little Red Fellow wouldn't give Conal either aise or peace till he consented to go. And he was so insistent that he pushed Conal before him till they came to France, and came to the King of France's castle. There the Wee Red Man knocked on the gates of the castle, and a soldier comin' out asked them who they were, and what they wanted.

Says the Wee Red Man, "This is my master, Conal O'Donnell, the most famous doctor in all Ireland, come here to cure your King."

And when the soldier took a look at the famous doctor, he drew his sword, and with the flat of the sword began wallopin' both of them away.

But that instant there was a window thrown up in the castle, and who but the Queen herself, stuck her head out of the window, and called to the soldier what it was he was drivin' these two people away for?

Says the soldier, lookin' up at her, "These two ragged impostures would pretend that one of them is a famous doctor, come to cure the King."

"Oh, don't drive them away, don't drive them away," says she. "When all the greatest doctors in the world have tried to cure him, and have failed, they can't anyhow do worse than the greatest doctor of them all. Bring them in," says she, "and let them have a try, anyhow."

And the soldier led the two of them into the castle,

and up to the King's bedchamber. There was the King lying there, a horrid sight. All the greatest doctors in the world had tried their hand on him, and he was only worse after every doctor; and now he was given up and was dying entirely. The Queen and all the court filled the room, cryin' over him, trying to keep up his heart while he was dyin'.

When the soldier pushed the two lads into the chamber, the Queen, with clasped hands, ran toward them.

"Oh," says she, "do you think you can cure my King for me?"

The Wee Red Man stepped between her and Conal, saying, "Yes, madam, my master he thinks little about curin' a dozen Kings before breakfast-time."

She asked him what necessities his master required to help him cure the King, and the Wee Red Man ordered first a pot of boiling water be brought in and hung on the fire in the bedchamber—which was instantly done. Then he said his master was shy about curin' Kings when people were around; they must all leave the room. The Queen and all the court trooped out of the room, while the Little Red Man closed the door, and turned the key in it.

When Conal found himself and the Little Red Man

left alone with the dying King, he began to shake and
to shiver, and, "What—what—what is it you're up to
now?" says Conal, says he.

Says the Little Red Man, "You hold your tongue,
and do as I tell ye. Look around ye, Conal, and get
me a carvin' knife."

The two hands of Conal went up in the air, as he
shouted, "No, no, no! No more of your carvin' knives
for me!"

But the Little Red Man commanded Conal so that
he had to obey. And Conal had to search, and find,
and carry in the carvin' knife, that was droppin' out
of his shakin' fingers, as he fetched it to him. Then
the Little Red Man stooped down to the hearthstone,
and sharpened up the carvin' knife, and sharpened
it up, and sharpened it up, till the edge of it could
only be fingered very jinteely.

Then, while Conal was lookin' on, shakin' and
shiverin' with his two knees knockin' together, the
Little Red Man went over to the bed, where the King
was lyin' dying, took hold of the King by the hair of
the head, and cut the head off him. He carried it over
and put it in the kettle of boilin' water on the fire.

"Now, Conal," says he, "look about ye and get a
stick and stir the King's head in the pot.

But Conal had collapsed in a chair.

"No, no," he groaned. "I'll have no hand in this murder."

"Hold your tongue," says the Little Red Man, "and do as I tell ye!" And Conal, behold ye, had to get hold of a stick, and begin stirrin' the King's head in the pot. And as he stirred, and stirred, and stirred, the head melted and melted and melted, till at length it melted away complete!

Then Conal collapsed. "And now," says he, "our lives are lost, anyhow!"

"Hold your tongue," says the Little Red Fellow, says he, "and get up and go on stirring the pot!"

And Conal had to begin again stirrin' away and stirrin' away, and, behold ye, he hadn't been another minute stirrin' when he beheld a new little head beginnin' to come in the pot. And as he stirred away and stirred away, the head grew away and grew away, till at length it was the full size. And then the Little Red Fellow, comin' over, and lookin' in, said, "I think it's done, now."

He lifted the head out of the pot, and stuck the head on the King, in the bed. And that instant the King sat up in his bed, and began talkin', and chattin', and laughin', completely cured, the Queen with screams of joy, first embraced and kissed the King. And with her arms wide, she ran at Conal.

"No, ma'am, thank you," says Conal, says he,

raisin' his hand against her, "I've a wife of me own at home."

On her knees then she fell with hands clasped, to thank Conal from the bottom of her heart. "You're surely," says she, "the most famous doctor the world ever knew. And," says she, "I'll give you your weight in gold every year, if you remain and be the King's doctor for the remainder of your days."

"No, ma'am," says Conal, says he. "The people at home in Ireland will be dyin', and I must hurry home to cure them. Get me up my five bags of gold."

The Queen had the butler get up the five bags of gold out of the cellar. And the Little Red Fellow got the bags on his back, and off for Ireland both of them set.

When they had traveled three days and three nights, the Little Red Fellow looked down at his shoes, saw that they were badly worn, with his ten toes stickin' out through them.

And, "Conal," says he, "will you buy me a new pair of shoes?"

Now when Conal was a poor man, he was, as you remimber, the best-hearted man in all the world, would divide his last bit of bread with his enemy. But now that he was a rich man, his nature was completely changed. And he answered back the Little Red Fellow: "No, the times is hard, and money scarce, and

I can't afford you any shoes. The ones you have will do you well enough. Go on and carry home my gold to Ireland."

And the instant he showed himself a bad fellow the Little Red Man, with the five bags of gold upon his back, rose up into the air, and disappeared through the skies, leavin' Conal upon the road, alone and lonely, poorer than he had ever been in all his life afore!

Conal's heart sank into his shoes, and he went stumblin' along the road, wonderin' what he'd do, at all, at all. Next minute his hangin' head struck again' somethin', and, behold ye, it was a post on the roadside, and there was a placard on the post. And Conal looked up to see what it was the placard said.

And, behold ye, what it said was that the King of Spain was dying. All the greatest doctors in the world had tried to cure him, but they had all failed, and the Queen was now offering ten bags of gold to any doctor in all the world who could cure the King.

For joy, Conal clapped his hands, and said, "Now my fortune's made, for now I know how to cure Kings." And off he started runnin', and never stopped till he was in Spain, and at the King's castle, and rattling on the gate.

And when he told the soldier who came out, that he was the famous Irish doctor, Conal O'Donnell, the soldier cried out: "Why, we've been searchin' all the world for you. The Queen heard how you cured the King of France, and was screengin' the earth's corners to get you. Come in, come in!" And he led Conal up to the King's bedchamber, where the Queen and all the court filled the room. And the King, given up by all the greatest doctors, was dyin' entirely.

When the soldier led Conal in, and announced that he was the famous Irish doctor, Conal O'Donnell, come to cure the King, the Queen almost fainted for joy, and threw herself on her knees before Conal, and begged, "Oh, great Irish doctor, do you think you can cure my King for me?"

"Ma'am," says Conal, says he, "I'll make short work of your man for you."

She then asked him what he required to help cure the King. And what he wanted was a pot of boiling water to be hung upon the fire, and then all the people to leave the room. Both of these things were soon done, and he had the door locked behind them.

Then, when he was left alone with the dying King, the first thing he did, naturally, was to look for a carvin' knife. And then, stooping down by the hearth-stone, he sharpened up the carvin' knife, and sharpened it up, and sharpened it up, till he had a fine jinteel point upon the carvin' knife. And then, taking the dying King by the hair o' the head, he cut the head off the King, and dropped the head into the pot of boiling water on the fire, and getting a stick, began stirrin' the King's head in the pot. As he stirred away and stirred away, the head melted away and melted away, until at length the head completely disappeared.

"It's doin' fine," says Conal. "It's half done now."

And then he went on stirrin' away and watchin' away, and stirrin' away and watchin' away, but, behold ye, if he had been stirrin' away and watchin' away from that day to this, he couldn't get any new head to come in the pot.

And after an hour of this the Queen and the court began beatin' at the doors, to get in, and there was the King lyin' on the bed, without a head on him!

Conal, he collapsed on the floor, cryin', "Now, my life is done, anyhow, and right well I do deserve it."

Just at that very instant wasn't there a tip-tap-tipping at the window. And lookin' over, who should he see but the Little Red Man perched on the window-sill wantin' to get in.

In three shakes of a lamb's lug, Conal had the window thrown up, and the Little Red Man had hopped into the room. And snatchin' the stick from Conal's hand, he began stirrin' the pot.

And, behold ye, he hadn't given three stirs to the pot when Conal looked in and saw a new little head begin to come in the pot! And three stirs more, and, behold ye, the head was full size! Then the Little Red Man looked in and said, "I think it's done now."

And taking the head from the pot, he went over and stuck the head on the King in the bed, and that instant the King sat up, and began chattin' and talkin' and laughin', completely cured, better than ever he'd been in all of his born days. Then the Wee Red Fellow said, "Conal, I'll wait for you outside," and hopped out of the window.

When Conal opened the door, and the Queen and the court came in, and saw the King sittin' up, and talkin' and chattin' and laughin' in bed, the Queen, overcome with joy, embraced and kissed the King, and then fell on her knees before Conal, thankin' him from the bottom of her heart, and offerin' him three times his weight in gold, as a salary every year, if he'd remain and be the King's doctor for the remainder of his life.

But Conal was tremblin' in his skin for fear that the King should take it in his mind to sneeze, and the head of him come bouncin' on the floor again, before he paid.

When he went out, the Little Red Man got the ten bags of gold upon his back, and off they started home for Ireland. Three days and three nights they traveled before them, and on the fourth day the Little

Red Man looked down at his shoes, saw that they were badly worn, with his ten toes stickin' out through them, and he said, "Conal, buy me a new pair of shoes."

Says Conal, says he, "Go buy yourself a hundred thousand pairs of shoes. The money is yours, and not mine. It is you that have earned it, and it is you that has the right to spend it all for whatsoever you please."

"Why, Conal," says the Wee Red Man, "you are your own good-hearted self again. Now," says he, "I want no shoes from you; I want none of your gold. I want nothing, for I'm one of the gentle people, the fairies, and anything in the world I want, I've only to wish for, and I'll have it. I only asked you that to test you. Now that you're your own good-hearted self, the gold is yours, and I'll carry it home for you to Ireland."

And off they started, and never stopped, halted, nor paused, till they reached Ireland, and reached the top of the hill above Conal's own house, where they see Conal's house and forge lying in the valley below.

There the Little Red Man laid down the ten bags of gold to Conal, and he said, "Now, Conal, you're the wealthiest, and happiest man in all Ireland. Good-bye, good luck to you, and God bless you!" And rising up in the air, he disappeared through the skies.

Conal looked at his ten bags of gold, and said:

"Now I'm the wealthiest man in all Ireland, and I'm the happiest— Oh, no," says he, as old memories flashed on him, "I'm not happy! Sure the King of Ireland will behead me for killin' his horse, and after that they'll hang me for murderin' my wife and my mother-in-law. Sure," says he, "instead of being the happiest, it's the miserablest divil I am, in all Ireland."

And a doleful eye he cast down to his house, in the valley below. And there, behold ye, first thing he saw was the King of Ireland's beautiful dancin', prancin', yellow steed, standin' up outside his forge, with a new set of legs under him, and a new set of shoes to them. And the next thing he beheld was his wife and his mother-in-law alive and well, comin' runnin' out of the house to greet him. With a joyful cry, he hoisted the ten bags of gold on his back, and went galloping down the hillside.

And, behold ye, when he met his wife and his mother-in-law, he found that they were not only alive and well, but both of them had grown young and beautiful—and, what is more than all else besides, both of them were grown good-tempered once again.

Conal, all rejoiced, went home with his arms around them, and next day, in his joy, he married his wife again. And he asked all the worl' to the weddin'. And that was the greatest weddin' ever known before or since. It lasted nine days and nine nights, and the last day and night was better than the first. And Conal built a castle with a window for every day in the year, where he and his wife, and his mother-in-law lived happy and well, ever after.

ACKNOWLEDGMENT

THE AUTHOR AND PUBLISHER wish to make acknowledgment of their indebtedness to the following publishers:

To Coward-McCann, Inc., for permission to use: "The Drawbridge" from *Not Really!* by Lesley Frost, copyright 1939 by Coward-McCann, Inc.

To Doubleday, Doran & Company, Inc., for permission to use: "Conal and Donal and Taig" from *Donegal Fairy Stories* by Seumas MacManus, copyright 1900 by Doubleday, Doran & Company, Inc.; "Mr. A and Mr. P" from *A Street of Little Shops* by Margery Bianco, copyright 1932, courtesy of Doubleday, Doran & Company, Inc.

To E. P. Dutton & Company, Inc., for permission to use: "Ah Mee's Invention" from *Shen of the Sea* by Arthur Bowie Chrisman, published and copyright by E. P. Dutton & Company, Inc., New York.

To Harcourt, Brace and Company, Inc., for permission to use: "The Laughing Prince" from *The Laughing Prince*, copyright 1921 by Parker Fillmore; "The Devil's Hide" from *Mighty Mikko,* copyright 1922 by Parker Fillmore.

To Harper & Brothers, for permission to use: "The Three Innkeepers" from *Spider's Palace* by Richard Hughes; "The Palace on the Rock" from *Don't Blame Me* by Richard Hughes; "Rats" from *My Friend, Mr Leakey* by J. B. S. Haldane; "The Simpleton and His Little Black Hen" from *Wonder Clock* by Howard Pyle.

To Houghton Mifflin Company, for permission to use: "The Peterkins Try to Become Wise" from *The Peterkin*

Acknowledgment]

Papers by Lucretia P. Hale; "About Elizabeth Eliza's Piano" from *The Peterkin Papers* by Lucretia P. Hale.

To G. P. Putnam's Sons, for permission to use: "Gudbrand on the Hill-side" from *East o' the Sun and West o' the Moon* translated by G. W. Dasent, courtesy of G. P. Putnam's Sons.

To Random House, for permission to use: "The Ghost's Ghost" from *Mouseknees* by William C. White, copyright 1939 by Random House, Inc., reprinted by special permission of the publishers.

To Ruth Sawyer, for permission to use: "Juan Cigarron."

To Frederick A. Stokes Company, for permission to use: "The Wee Red Man" from *Donegal Wonder Book* by Seumas MacManus, copyright 1926 by Frederick A. Stokes Company.

To *Story Parade*, for permission to use: "Baby Rainstorm" by Glen Rounds, "How Pat Got Good Sense" by Charles J. Finger, and "Ebenezer Never-Could-Sneezer" by Gilbert S. Pattillo.

A NOTE ON THE TYPE

This book was set on the Linotype in "Baskerville," a facsimile of the type designed, in 1754, by John Baskerville, a writing-master of Birmingham, England. This type was one of the forerunners of the "modern" style of type faces. The Linotype copy was cut under the supervision of George W. Jones of London.